Egon
Werlich

Student's Guide to Text Production

Cornelsen

StD Dr. Egon Werlich

Student's Guide to Text Production

Umschlagentwurf: Knut Waisznor

1. Auflage Druck 8 7 6 5 Jahr 02 01 2000 99
Alle Drucke dieser Auflage können im Unterricht nebeneinander verwendet werden.

Satz MEDIA trend, Berlin
Druck Druck-Centrum Fürst, Berlin

ISBN 3-464-02029-0

Bestellnummer 20290

gedruckt auf säurefreiem Papier, umweltschonend
hergestellt aus chlorfrei gebleichten Faserstoffen

Table of Contents

Vorwort

Ziele des „Guide“

Der vorliegende Band ist als Wegweiser und Begleiter *(guide)* für Schüler/innen gedacht, die mehr Sicherheit im Verfassen englischer Texte erlangen wollen. Er kann ab Klasse 10 im Englischunterricht benutzt werden, unter Anleitung des Lehrers oder im Selbststudium.

Ziel der ab Klasse 9 einsetzenden Sprachausbaustufe ist, bis zum Ende der Klasse 13 zunehmend freier und zusammenhängend in der Fremdsprache reden und schreiben zu können. Mit den gewohnten Hilfsmitteln für den Englischunterricht - alphabetischen Wörterbüchern und speziellen Grammatiken - läßt sich dieses Ziel allerdings kaum erreichen. Wer nämlich z. B. kurze Vorträge anhand von Notizen halten will, dezidiert seine Meinung in Gesprächen einbringen möchte oder Interpretationen von Texten schreiben soll, muß zunächst die jeweils benötigte Textform kennen und die entsprechenden Redemittel zur Verfügung haben.

Dieser „Guide“ zeigt einen einfachen und zugleich sicheren Weg, wie die unterschiedlichen Typen und Ausdrucksformen des Sprechens und Schreibens zu unterscheiden sind und welcher Wortschatz, welche Strukturen und welche Regeln der Textbildung jeweils benötigt werden.

Funktion des Einleitungskapitels (Part I)

Zu Beginn des Bandes werden sieben einfache Regeln dargestellt, die man beachten sollte, wann immer man zusammenhängend sprechen oder schreiben will. Sie können bei der Durchnahme der folgenden Kapitel stets schnell nachgeschlagen und wiederholt werden.

Einfache Orientierung an zwölf Textformen (Part II)

Der „Guide“ geht von den fünf grundlegenden Typen des Sprechens und Schreibens in Texten aus: Beschreiben *(description)*, Erzählen *(narration)*, Erklären *(exposition)*, Argumentieren *(argumentation)* und Anweisen *(instruction)*. Diesen Grundverfahren werden hier insgesamt zwölf Textformen zugeordnet, z. B. Geschichten *(stories)*, Textzusammenfassungen *(summaries)*, Berichte *(reports)*, Stellungnahmen *(comments)* oder Textinterpretationen *(text interpretations)*. Diese Textformen stellen die wichtigsten Ausdrucksformen für unser Sprechen und Schreiben in zusammenhängenden Texten dar. Weitere Varianten wie Nachrichten *(news stories)*, Geschäftsbriefe *(business letters)*, Referate *(term papers)* oder Leitartikel *(leading articles)* können auf dieser Grundlage ebenfalls erklärt werden.

Anhand von konkreten Beispielen erfahren die Schüler/innen in Part II, welche charakteristischen Merkmale die einzelnen Textformen aufweisen. In einzelnen leicht faßbaren Schritten lernen sie dann, selbst unterschiedliche Textformen zu konzipieren. Die hier präsentierten Textformen sind nicht nur hilfreich für die Arbeit im Englischunterricht, sondern leisten auch in den meisten Schulfächern und später im Studium und Berufsleben gute Dienste.

Eine wichtige Lernerleichterung für das Schreiben (Part III)

Wer z. B. einen *comment* schreiben will und sich in Part II über den Aufbau dieser Textform informiert hat, braucht noch Wortschatz- und Grammatikhilfen zur konkreten Ausformulierung. Ein reichhaltiges Angebot an Formulierungsvorschlägen hält das *text form dictionary* (Part III) bereit, das auf die 12 Abschnitte in Part II genau abgestimmt ist.

Dieses neuartige Textformwörterbuch bietet Wörter in ihren wichtigsten Wortverbindungen *(collocations)* und mit den benötigten grammatischen Anschlüssen, so daß das Umsetzen von Sprechabsichten in Sätze und Abschnitte in der jeweils gewünschten Textform leicht gemacht wird.

Die Sprache des „Guide“

In den Kapiteln dieses „Guide“ wird durchgehend nur ein leicht verständliches Englisch zur Erläuterung und Erklärung verwandt. Für möglicherweise dennoch unbekannte Wörter (das gilt vor allem für die wichtigen authentischen Beispieltexte) werden die deutschen Entsprechungen in Klammern angeboten. Der Gebrauch von Fachbegriffen in den Erklärungen ist auf ein Mindestmaß beschränkt, so daß das Behalten des Wesentlichen erleichtert und nicht zusätzlich erschwert wird.

Der „Guide“ zur Schulung für bessere Textanalyse

Wer die typischen Ordnungen, Schritte und Formulierungen beim Verfassen einzelner Textformen kennt, nimmt beim Zuhören und Lesen auch differenzierter bestimmte Signale in Texten wahr. Das Wissen darum, mit welchen Redewendungen und Aufbautechniken z. B. ein *summary* geschrieben wird, ermöglicht es beim Lesen oder Zuhören des *summary* eines anderen Verfassers, die dort verpackten Informationen leichter zu entschlüsseln. Mit anderen Worten, Kenntnisse über die Textproduktion erweisen sich auch als hilfreich bei der Textrezeption.

Zum Gebrauch des „Guide" beim Schreiben

Der „Guide" sollte zielgerichtet eingesetzt werden.

Beispiele:
- Durchnahme einer neuen Textform in der Klasse/im Kurs: Gemeinsames Lesen des Einleitungskapitels (Part I), dann Erarbeitung der gerade benötigten Textform im Plenum (betreffende Stellen in Part II und Part III). In Klasse 10 könnte dies ein *summary*, in Klasse 11 ein *comment* sein.
- individuelle Vorbereitung auf Klassenarbeiten/Klausuren: Wiederholung des Einleitungskapitels (Part I), dann Konzentration z. B. auf die Textform *text interpretation* (betreffende Stellen in Part II und Part III). Je nach Anforderung mit zusätzlicher Aufnahme von Querverweisen auf *definition, explication, summary* oder *comment.*
- individuelle Bearbeitung schriftlicher Übungen, insbesondere Hausaufgaben: Konzentration auf die Formulierungshilfen des Textformwörterbuchs (Part III), speziell die Abschnitte für den Textanfang, die Mitte bzw. den Schluß.

Einzelne Kapitel und Abschnitte des „Guide" wurden in einer Erprobungsphase mit Schülern des Max-Planck-Gymnasiums in Dortmund – darunter vielen ehemaligen Haupt- und Realschülern – über mehrere Jahre überprüft, vereinfacht und durch weitere Beispiele angereichert. Die Schüler, die nach den Prinzipien dieses „Guide" das Verfassen von englischen Texten gelernt haben, machten erfreuliche Fortschritte, teilweise auch in muttersprachlichen Fächern wie insbesondere Deutsch. Der vorliegende „Guide" ist geschrieben worden mit dem Wunsch des Verfassers, daß seine Benutzer – im Unterricht oder im Selbststudium – mit seiner Hilfe ebenso sicher und umfassend zu guten Sprech- und Schreiberfolgen gelangen mögen.

Dortmund, im Mai 1987 *E. Werlich*

Abbreviations and symbols

cf.	confer; compare (with), see
e.g.	exempli gratia; for example
fml.	formal
i.e.	id est; that is
infml.	informal
loc. cit.	loco citato; in the place cited
p., pp.	page, pages
sb.	somebody
sth.	something

⬒	beginning
⊟	middle
⬓	end

Part I

Seven simple rules for composing English texts

Rule 1

Write down the **topical keywords** (thematische Schlüsselwörter) that you can think of in connection with your subject (Gegenstand) or **theme** (umfassendes Thema). Put them down in a **list,** just as they come to your mind.
Start each topical note with a dash, like this:

Theme: North American peoples and cultures
- Who was there before recorded history began? → prehistory (Vorgeschichte)
- policies that the Europeans pursued (verfolgen) towards Indians
- characterization of Indians as an ethnic group (Volksgruppe) → the people

etc.

(FOR DETAILS, CF. II, 6.)

Rule 2

Read your list over once again when you cannot think of any more topical keywords. Try to give your first rough (grob) list some definite **order.** For instance, you might want to place the more important topical keywords last. Or you could start with the more particular topic and go over to a more general topic.
Add a number to each of the dashes to fix your new order.

2 Who was there before recorded history began? → prehistory
3 policies that the Europeans pursued towards Indians
1 characterization of Indians as an ethnic group → the people
etc.

Copy the numbered list in this new order. Try to write each topical note as a **heading** (Überschrift), so that you get a **topic outline** for your text. (FOR DETAILS, CF. II, 6.)

1. The people
2. Prehistory
3. Policies of Europeans towards Indians

etc.

Rule 3

Do not at first think of individual sentences, adding one after the other. Start from one of the topics of your outline (CF. "RULE 2") and think of composing one or more **paragraphs** for each topic. This topic can help you to write the first sentence for a paragraph, i.e. the **topic sentence.** The simplest plan for a paragraph of about five to ten sentences is this:

Beginning	Topic sentence (Themasatz)
Middle	Developing sentences (entfaltende Sätze) that start from the opening topic sentence
End	Concluding sentence (Schlußsatz)

topic from your outline ▶ 2. Prehistory

topic sentence ▶
developing sentences ▶
concluding sentence ▶

There are not many records of how and when North America was filled with people. / The earliest cultures can only generally be defined as hunting and gathering communities. These ancestors (Vorfahren) of the native Americans originally came from Asia. They began crossing from Asia into Alaska about thirty or forty thousand years ago, using the thousand-mile wide land bridge that appeared when the oceans fell some 300 feet during the Ice Age. They came in a series of migrations, perhaps following herds eastward whenever the Bering Sea sank and the land mass rose. The last great wave of settlers reached America about eight thousand years ago. By that time, those who had come before were spreading to the east and south from Alaska. / Some 25,000 years after their invasion began, they had taken possession of all of North and South America.

Rule 4

When you compose a longer text, for instance, part of a long text interpretation (cf. II, 9), you may want to use a special paragraph for the beginning, i.e. the **introduction,** and another special paragraph for the end, i.e. the **conclusion** (Schluß[abschnitt]). The introduction and the conclusion can strongly support the order of all the paragraphs in between (dazwischen).
Your text, then, will be similar in composition to an individual paragraph (cf. "Rule 3").

Beginning	Introductory paragraph
Middle	Developing paragraphs
End	Concluding paragraph

Use your introductory paragraph, for instance, to mention the number of topics that you will deal with. This will help you to give your text a **listing order** (cf. II, 6). Or use your introduction to mention an inclusive term (umfassender Begriff) before you turn to the individual elements. This will help you to give your text an **analytical order** (cf. II, 4–9).

In my report on the North American peoples and cultures, I shall deal with three main aspects. First I shall characterize the people – the basic physical type they represent, their numbers and languages, and the main culture areas in which groups of tribes are to be found. In a second step I shall look at the earliest history of settlers in North America, the prehistory of North American Indians. Thirdly, and lastly, I shall look at European policies towards Indians, from the beginning of the discovery of the continent to the present day.

The most important purpose of your concluding paragraph should be to announce the end of your text. You may want to sum up your results (CF. II, 7). Or you might choose to introduce the last numbered topic of your list (CF. II, 6). Or you could mention the important or surprising element of some matter (CF. II, 2).

To sum up our survey of the prehistory and recorded history of North American peoples and cultures, we can perhaps say that...

Rule 5

In each of your paragraphs on a topic, connect your sentences. You can do this by choosing again expressions which are clearly linked with the topical keyword in your topic sentence. The reader must be able to recognize this **topical coherence** (thematischer Zusammenhang) in your paragraph (CF. "RULE 3").

In Hemingway's story "At Two o'clock in the Morning", Drevitts comments on **Boyle's shooting of the two Hungarians,** "*That*'s all right maybe this time." In my view, however, *Boyle* should be strongly condemned for *his way of acting*. Surely, *Boyle does not care* about the law of the country, etc. (CF. II, 10)

You can also connect your sentences by using signals which show your reader whether you are describing something, telling a story, explaining something, commenting on some problem, or giving instructions on how to do something (CF. "TEXT FORM DICTIONARY", III, 1–12). In the example above, all the connecting signals show that the writer is commenting on the problem of how to evaluate (bewerten) "Boyle's shooting of the two Hungarians":

In Hemingway's story "At Two o'clock in the Morning", Drevitts **comments** on Boyle's shooting of the two Hungarians, "*That's all right maybe* this time." **In my view,** *however,* Boyle should be *strongly condemned* for his way of acting. *Surely,* Boyle does not care about the law of the country, etc. (CF. II, 10)

In long texts, also use signals which refer back over long distances to the topics of groups of paragraphs that have gone before. These **long-distance signals** can help you to keep the composition of a long text clear. You might write, for example, at the end of one group of paragraphs:

There is, in short, an *element of make-believe* (Schein) in literature.

Later, perhaps at the beginning of a new group of paragraphs, you could refer to that thought like this:

> In addition to *this element/the above-mentioned element of make-believe,* there is in literature – as opposed to other compositions of words – also great importance in the arrangements (Anordnungen) of sound and in the richness of suggestion (Andeutung, Bedeutung; CF. II, 5).

Rule 6

Make the whole composition of your longer texts clear (for yourself while writing, and for your reader or listener later) by using **headings** and **subheadings.** These headings can sum up and clearly point to the topics of a larger group of paragraphs in your composition.
You can choose your headings and subheadings from your own topic outline (CF. "RULES 2 AND 6). You may use the clipped (verkürzt) language of newspaper headlines (no articles, -ing forms of verbs, etc.; CF. II, 6), or you may use complete sentences, especially questions.

> [...]
> Boyle's use of his gun
> The first reason is connected with the particular situation in which Boyle uses his gun. Policemen carry guns chiefly because they must be able to defend themselves if they are threatened. Moreover, they may... (CF. II, 8)

Rule 7

In your longer texts, especially in text interpretations and long comments, learn also to combine the different **text forms** for different intentions (Absichten; CF. II, 1–12). For instance, use definitions, summaries, explications, and comments in clearly noticeable paragraphs or groups of paragraphs of a text interpretation (CF. II, 9). A linking introduction (überleitende Einleitung) with expressions from the "Text form dictionary" can greatly improve your text composition. Or use a technical description, a story or an explication as clearly signalled sections of a comment (CF. "TEXT FORM DICTIONARY", III, 1–12). You may, for instance, begin with a short **comment:**

> *I think that* Drevitts markedly (['mɑ:kɪdlɪ], deutlich) differs from Boyle. Drevitts's choice of words in his comment in line ... *clearly* shows that he fears they will be held responsible and will perhaps even be charged with the killings.

Then you continue with a **text interpretation** as evidence for your view:

> When Drevitts says to Boyle, "You oughtn't to have done it" (l. ...), his choice of the auxiliary "oughtn't to" points to a moral obligation (Verpflichtung). *Similarly,* when he says, "There's *liable to* be a hell of a lot of trouble" (l. ...), "be liable" *indicates that* he knows that these killings cannot be easily justified (rechtfertigen) by them before their superiors (Vorgesetzte) or before a lawcourt.

And then you may take up your **comment** again like this:

> *I think* in the illustrated reactions Drevitts can be seen to differ very strongly from his companion. Drevitts knows and feels obliged (verpflichtet) to respect the law of the country. (CF. II, 10)

Part II

Text forms

Descriptive text forms

In descriptive ([dɪ'skrɪptɪv], beschreibend) texts we show what objects, scenes, or persons in space ([uns umgebender] Raum) look like. Descriptive texts often form part of a longer text, especially of a long story (CF. II, 2).
Examples of **impressionistic descriptions** ([persönlich gefärbte] Schilderungen) are stage directions (Bühnenanweisungen) in plays, parts of character sketches such as the profiles (['prəʊfaɪlz], [Personen] Porträts) in newspapers, parts of travel books and diaries (Tagebücher), of poems and of novels (Romane).
Technical descriptions (['teknɪkəl], Sachbeschreibungen), on the other hand, are written from an objective point of view of what objects, scenes, or persons look like.
To order the details of a descriptive text, writers will always refer to positions (Lagen), locations (Standorte), and directions ([dɪ'rekʃənz], Richtungen).

1. Impressionistic and technical descriptions

Definition: In descriptions generally, we look at a thing or person from a fixed viewpoint (Blickwinkel) in space. So we usually first refer to the place where something is to be found, and from there we follow a particular direction in space. We can move, for instance,
- from left to right,
- from high to low,
- from front to back,
- from outside to inside, or
- from near to far.

In other words, we follow and show a spatial order (räumliche Anordnung) of things in descriptive texts.
We write an **impressionistic description** when we present our subjective impressions (persönliche Eindrücke) of what objects, scenes, or persons look like. We then choose our words so that they express our dominant (vorherrschend) feelings, mood (Stimmung) or reactions to what we see. "A magnificent (großartig) building" expresses our feelings, "a three-storey (dreigeschossig) building" does not. To evoke (heraufbeschwören) a certain impression, we can also use comparisons (Vergleiche), metaphors (Metaphern, als Bild verkürzte Vergleiche), or exaggerations ([ɪɡˌzædʒə'reɪʃnz], Übertreibungen).
In **technical descriptions,** on the other hand, we try to show an object or a scene as it really is. We are not interested in what a thing or scene means to us personally. So we use exact references ([ɪɡ'zækt], genaue Verweise) to detail: to the size (Größe), measurements (['meʒəmənts], Maße), colours, or qualities (Eigenschaften) of things in space. Words that express our subjective impressions ("a *magnificent* building") are avoided in a technical description ("a *three-storey* building").
In order to give precise and accurate information in a technical description, we must also know some of the technical terms (Fachausdrücke) that an expert would use. Sometimes, we can also use an illustration, e. g. a drawing (Zeichnung) or a diagram, to make understanding of the described object easier for our reader.

Forms

The following texts illustrate how we can write a subjective or an objective description:

1) An **impressionistic description** which the American writer Mark Twain once gave of the city of Heidelberg:

▭ Behind the Castle *swells* (sich aufwölben) a great domeshaped (kuppelförmig) hill, *forest-clad* and beyond that a *nobler* and *loftier* one. ⊟ The Castle looks down upon the compact brown-roofed town; and from the town two *picturesque* (malerisch) old bridges span the river. Now the view broadens; through the *gateway* (Tor) of the *sentinel headlands* (Wache stehende Hügelausläufer) you gaze out over the wide Rhine plain, which stretches away, softly and richly tinted (getönt), grows gradually and *dreamily* indistinct ◻ and finally *melts* (schmelzen) imperceptibly (unmerklich) into the remote (fern) horizon.

(Mark Twain, *A Tramp Abroad.* London, 1880, pp. 12 f.)

▭ Beginning

a) A fixed viewpoint *("the Castle")* and the direction from near to far (here *"Behind the Castle", "and beyond"*)

⊟ Middle

b) The fixed viewpoint and the direction from high to low (here: *"looks down upon", "and from the town", "the view broadens"*)

c) Use of adjectives that express the writer's subjective reactions (here: "nobler and loftier", "picturesque", etc.)

d) Use of images to support a dominant impression (here: *"gateway", "sentinel headlands"*)

◻ End

e) Use of a closing signal ("and finally") and reference to the end of the described scene (here: *"the remote horizon"*)

2) A largely **technical description** of the area that a city covers:

▭ Hiroshima was *a fan-shaped* (fächerförmig) *city, lying* mostly *on* the six islands formed by the seven estuarial rivers (Mündungsflüsse) that *branch out* (sich verzweigen) from the Ota River; ⊟ its main commercial and residential *districts* (Handels- und Wohnbezirke), *covering* about *four square miles in the centre of* the city, *contained* three-quarters of its population, which had been reduced (verringern) by several evacuation (Umsiedlung) programmes from a wartime peak (Spitze) of 380,000 to about 245,000. Factories and other residential *districts* (Wohnbezirke), or *suburbs* (Vororte), *lay compactly* (dicht zusammengedrängt) *around the edges of* the city. *To the south*

▭ Beginning

a) An inclusive expression for a position, shape (Gestalt, Form), or direction in space (here: "fan-shaped", "city"; at the end: "delta"). Use of a comparison in "fan-shaped" ("shaped *like* a fan")

⊟ Middle

b) Use of space words for one direction, so that a spatial order is formed (here, from near to far: "in the centre", "around the edges", "To the south")

c) Use of verbs that refer to spatial position or direction (here: "lie", "branch out", "cover", "contain", "run around", "studded"). Here connected with exact references to size ("four square miles", etc.)

d) Use of adjectives that refer to spatial position or forms (here: "fan-shaped", "residential", "compact")

e) Use of nouns that refer to spatial position or direction (here: "the edges of", "a rim of", "sides of")

were the docks, an airport, and an *island-studded* (mit Inseln übersät) Inland Sea. ◻ *A rim of* mountains (Gebirgsrand) *runs around* the other three *sides of the delta.*

(John Hersey, *Hiroshima*, Harmondsworth, 1946, p. 17)

f) Reference to the four points of the compass (Himmelsrichtungen) when a scene or an area is described

◻ End:
g) Inclusive expressions for a spatial observation (here: "a rim", "runs around", "the delta")

3) A partly **impressionistic description** of a room to characterize its owners, the family of Princess Margaret, the sister of Queen Elizabeth II:

◻ They have one spare (zusätzlich) bedroom, and *the house* is *not so lavish* (verschwenderisch angelegt) as the rebuilding price indicates (andeuten). ◻ *The drawing room* (Wohnzimmer) is *a short way down the corridor, on the right* as you *enter* the building. It is *long, large,* and *looks on to* (mit Blick auf) a garden. *In the centre, at right angles to* the fireplace (Kamin), are two large sofas, one with a children's comic in the middle. A *low* stool (Hocker) *holds* neatly *stacked* (säuberlich aufgestapelt) magazines and large books, including Snowdon's "Private View". *Behind the sofa* is a drink trolley (Servierwagen) and, *opposite* (gegenüber), a desk *jumbled with* (wahllos übersät mit) papers. *Underneath the desk* is a shopping basket (Einkaufskorb) and handbag. ◻ Small trinkets (Kinkerlitzchen), objets d'art (Kunstgegenstände), are *cluttered around* (verstreut herumliegen) *the room* complementing the Anthony Fry pictures.

(Andrew Duncan, "The Snowdons", *The Observer*, 10 May 1970)

◻ Beginning
a) An inclusive expression for position, shape, or direction (here: "the house"). Giving a dominant impression (here: "not so lavish")

◻ Middle
b) Use of space words for one direction, so that a spatial order is formed (here: from outside to inside)
c) Spatial order through adjectives that refer to shape or size (here: "short", "long", "large", "low")
d) Spatial order through adverbials of place (Ortsadverbiale; here: "on the right", "in the centre", "at right angles to")
e) Spatial order through adverbs of place (here: "opposite"), adverbials of place (here: "*behind* the sofa", "*underneath* the desk", etc.) and other space words ("low", "holds", etc.)
f) Lively description through verbs of movement (Bewegungsverben) for directions in space (here: "as you *enter*")
g) Lively description through verbs of sight (Verben des Sehens) for directions in space (here: "look on to")

◻ End
h) An inclusive expression for a spatial impression (here: "cluttered around the room")

4) A **technical description** of an object:

◻ The photographic *camera* is shown in Fig. 71 [...]. ◻ It uses a convex lens *at one end of* a lightproof box. Rays of light from the object *enter* the lens. After being bent or refracted (gebrochen) the rays *form* an inverted (umge-

◻ Beginning
a) An inclusive expression for position, shape, or direction (here: "the camera")

◻ Middle
b) Use of space words for one direction, so that a spatial order is formed (here: from "one

kehrt) image *at the other end of* the box. The image *appears* on a film or glass plate that is coated (überzogen) with a compound (Zusammensetzung) of silver extremely sensitive to light (lichtempfindlich). ◻ In most cameras the lens is mounted (eingebaut) at the front of *a movable bellows* (Blasebalg) to permit proper (angemessen) focusing (Scharfeinstellung) of objects at different distances.

end" to "the other end", and from outside to inside)
c) Lively description through verbs that show changes in space (here: "enter", "form", "appear")
d) Use of a neutral style: no personal impressions or opinions
e) Use of some technical terms that an expert needs (here: "photographic", "convex lens", "refracted", "inverted", "coated", "compound", "bellows", "focusing")

◻ End
f) The last detail of the described shape (here: "a movable bellows")

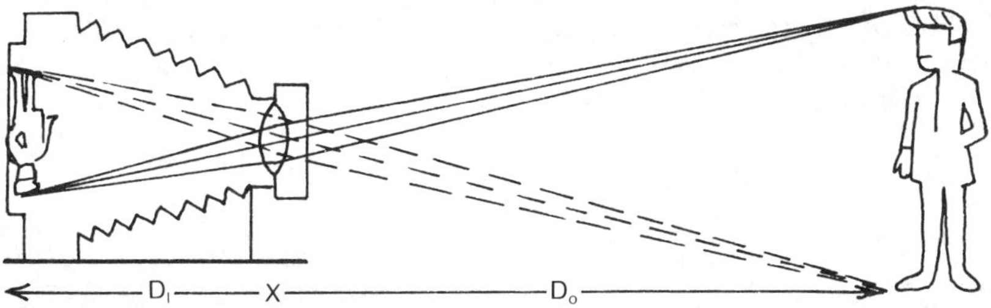

(LOUIS T. MASSON, *GENERAL SCIENCE MADE EASY*. NEW YORK, 1965, P. 137)

General steps for writing a descriptive text

1) Use an introduction with an **inclusive spatial expression** (umfassender, auf Raum bezogener Ausdruck) that shows the position, shape, or direction of something.

Hiroshima was *a fan-shaped city,* lying mostly on the six islands formed by the seven estuarial rivers that *branch out from* the Ota River.

*

2) Move on from your opening spatial expression by using further **space words** for one direction in your text, so that your text is given a **spatial order** (räumliche Ordnung). You can use:
a) simple **adverbs of place,** such as "here", "there", "over there" or "opposite". For instance: "Behind the sofa is a drink trolley and, *opposite*, a desk jumbled with papers";
b) **adverbials of place.** For instance: "*In the centre, at right angles to* the fireplace, are two large sofas"; or use
c) **local clauses** with "where" or "wherever" (wo[hin] auch immer). For instance: "*Wherever* you look in the room, you see small trinkets cluttered around."

You can also use:
d) **verbs** that refer to a position or direction in space. For instance: "its main commercial and residential districts, *covering* about four square miles in the centre of the city, *contained* three-quarters of its population";
e) **nouns** that refer to position or direction in space. For instance: "A *rim* of mountains runs around the other three *sides* of the *delta*"; or use
f) **adjectives** that refer to shape or size. For instance: "It [the drawing room] is *long, large,* and looks on to a garden."

3) To make your description lively, you can use **verbs of movement** ("enter", "come up to", "leave") and expressions that refer to **view or sight** ("look on to", "have a fine view of", "catch sight of"). For instance: "The drawing room is a short way down the corridor, on the right as you *enter* the building. It is long, large, and *looks on to* a garden."

4) Use the tenses of the **present tense group:** the present perfect, the present tense, will-future, and future perfect (CF. II, 2, "GENERAL STEPS", [5]). However, when your description is part of a story, use the tenses of the **past tense group** (CF. THE DESCRIPTION OF HIROSHIMA; CF. ALSO II, 2, "GENERAL STEPS", [4]).
(CF. "TEXT FORM DICTIONARY", III, 1.)

Some areas of use

The shorter forms of more or less technical descriptions can often be used as an elementary basis for telling others about the scene in a picture or a cartoon, as part of one's comment on it. A well-ordered description of the elements of the picture, and of how these are connected, can give the listener or reader a clear impression of the scene that he does not see himself. Here, for example, is a cartoon that went with an article on "The Dangers of Docudrama" in *Time* (FEB. 25, 1985):

An **interpretation** of the cartoon might begin like this:

> The cartoon appears to link up with the writer's highly critical comment that some docudramas "knowingly distort (verzerren) [...] the truth to advance (vorantreiben) a cause or enhance (herausstellen) a dramatic scene".

At some point in the interpretation there should be a **description** of the cartoon:

> The cartoon *scene* that is being filmed by a TV camera shows a man *on the right* pursuing another man *on the left*. The pursuer is threatening the pursued man with a dagger-like knife. The cameraman *at the TV camera,* however, has focused the camera in such a way that only *the central section of the scene* is shown *on the screen* (see the black sections of the men's bodies). This recorded scene completely reverses the roles of pursuer and pursued. *The scene on the screen* suggests that the man *on the left* is threatening the man *on the right* with a knife.

The end of the **interpretation** could read as follows:

> As Atlanta officials observed about the CBS show on the Atlanta child murders, this show is "simply wrong". The cartoonist appears to draw upon the technique that docudrama producers use, according to the writer: he exposes the abuse (Mißbrauch) of the possibilities that television has to distort the truth by being selective (auswählend).

Narrative text forms

In narrative (['nærətɪv], erzählend) text forms we speak about what happened in time. News stories in newspapers, short stories, novels, biographies, reports, anecdotes, fables, or jokes can all be grouped as narrative text forms or their variants. These text forms usually deal with what happened in a period of time that now belongs to the past.

2. Stories

Definition: In a story (Geschichte, Erzählung), we tell others about people's actions or about a series of events (Ereignisse) that happened at some time in the past. We usually mention the events as they happened in time, one after the other, i.e. in their chronological order. But we can also tell a story so that the most important or surprising action or event is mentioned right at the end, as a climax (Höhepunkt). Jokes, for instance, follow this climactic order (steigende Abfolge).
In more complex stories, those with a plot of opposed forces (durch Gegensätze ausgelöste Handlungskette), we can also show how actions and events happened as effects (Wirkungen) of certain causes (Ursachen). Fictional short stories or novels usually follow this cause-and-effect order. It is used to show the central meaning of a series of events. The events in the story of the Good Samaritan, for instance, show what it means to be a good neighbour.

Whatever story we tell, we speak (or: narrate [næˈreɪt]) from a personal (subjective) point of view. Another person may tell the story of what happened quite differently.

Forms

The following three texts illustrate how we can connect our sentences in stories when we follow a chronological order, a climactic order, or one of causes and effects.

1) A story from a diary (Tagebuch), told in a simple **chronological order:**

▭ December 24 – Cambridge
We had lunch on the terrace, talked, ▭ *and then* I had a nap *while* the President-elect [John F. Kennedy] and his father played golf. *Then* I went for a walk on the ocean side and talked with a Secret Service man who *was studying* beach crabs (Strandkrabben, -nixen) with the field glasses he had with him to spot approaching assassins (sich nähernde Attentäter). *Then* I met Caroline and the baby and talked *further* (weiter) with J. F. K. We were joined by Bob and Ethel for a family dinner. *Thereafter* I talked *again* with the President-elect and *at midnight* was driven back to the airport. I was somewhat tired and more so ▭ *when* I got to Boston *at breakfast time.*

(John Kenneth Galbraith, *Ambassador's Journal: A Personal Account of the Kennedy Years.* Signet, 1969, p. 27)

▭ Beginning
a) A situation: the time, place, persons and actions of an event

▭ Middle
b) Use of time adverbs that form a chronological order (here: "and then", "then", etc.)
c) Use of time clauses with "while", "when", or "as soon as" to show the chronological order
d) Use of the past continuous tense for short periods of time with a continuous action (here: "was studying")

▭ End
e) Use of a last reference to time (here "when ... at breakfast time")

2) A story with a **climactic order:**

▭ *This takes my mind back to years and years ago, when* a very young Member of Parliament was addressing a hostile meeting during a by-election in the north. ▭ A heckler (Zwischenrufer) shouted, "Does your mother know you're out?" And the young politician said, ▭ "Yes, and she'll very soon know that I'm in."

▭ Beginning
a) The situation in which the story is told ("This ...")
b) The narrated (erzählt) situation: the time, place, persons, and actions ("years and years ago, when ...")

▭ Middle
c) Use of, for instance, direct speech to lead up to the climax

▭ End
d) Use of a punch-line (Pointe) that introduces a surprise at the end

3) A plotted story in which a **cause-and-effect order** is added to the chronological and the climactic order:

▭ At two o'clock in the morning *two Hungarians got into a cigar store* at Fifteenth Street and Grand Avenue.

Drevitts and Boyle drove up from Fifteenth Street police station in a Ford.

▭ Beginning
a) An action in the situational introduction that becomes the *cause* of certain effects (see b). (Two Hungarians commit a burglary [Einbruch]. They become the first opposed force.)
b) A counter-action (Gegenhandlung) that comes as the *effect* of the action before (see a). (The police have been informed about the burglary. They become the second opposed force.)

▭ The Hungarians were backing their wagon out of an alley.

Boyle shot one off the seat of the wagon and one out of the wagon box.

▭ Middle
c) Another action (opposed force 1) that becomes the cause of further effects. (The burglars are about to leave the scene.)
d) The counter-action (opposed force 2) as an *effect*

Drevitts got frightened when he found they were both dead. "Hell, Jimmy," he said, "you oughtn't to have done it. There's liable to be a hell of a lot of trouble."

e) The effect in d) becomes the cause of a new *effect.* (Drevitts speaks up for force 1.)

"They're crooks, ain't they?" said Boyle. "They're wops, ain't they? Who the hell is going to make any trouble?"

f) The effect in e) becomes the cause of a new *effect.* (Boyle defends himself and indirectly threatens Drevitts.)

"That's all right maybe this time," said Drevitts, "but how did you know they were wops when you dumped them?"

g) The effect in f) becomes the cause of a new *effect.* (Drevitts becomes frightened of Boyle and backs down.)

▭ "Wops," said Boyle, "I can tell wops a mile off."

(Ernest Hemingway, *The Snows of Kilimanjaro and Other Stories.* Harmondsworth, 1963, p. 93)

▭ End
h) The effect of g) becomes the cause of a *final effect.* (Boyle does not feel that Drevitts is opposing him any longer and makes a joke.)

General steps for writing a story

1) Use an introduction in which you refer to a **situation** in the past. Mention the time, place, persons, and first action.

At two o'clock in the morning *(time)* two Hungarians *(persons)* got into (*first action* in the past tense) a cigar store at Fifteenth Street and Grand Avenue *(place)*.

2) If necessary, first link (verknüpfen) the story with the situation in which it is told. Use a **formulaic opening** (formelhafte Eröffnung), for instance:

This reminds me of a nice / funny / strange story about...
It makes me think of a short / little anecdote about...
That makes me think of my favourite joke about...

*

3) Move on from your opening time expression by using further **time words** in your text so that you form a **chronological order.** You can use:
a) a simple sequence (Abfolge) of **verbs in the past tense.** For instance: "Drevitts and Boyle *drove up* from... The Hungarians *were backing*..." (instead of: "*Then* Drevitts and Boyle drove up from...").
b) simple **time adverbs** for short jumps in time: "then", "later", "next", "now", "afterwards". For instance: "*Then* I went for a walk on the ocean side...".
c) **time adverbials:** "one day", "in the morning", "last year", "at midnight", "at six o'clock", etc. For instance: "...and *at midnight* [I] was driven back to the airport".
d) **time clauses** with "when", "while", "as soon as", "before", "after", "until", etc. For instance: "I was somewhat tired and more so *when I got to Boston at breakfast time*".

4) Use the tenses of the **past tense group** in most narrative text forms (an exception, for instance, is the sports report; it is told in the present tense group):

The past tense group

Past perfect	**Past tense**	**Conditional I**	**Conditional II**
I had been (Ich war gewesen)	I was (Ich war)	I should/would be (Ich würde sein/Ich wäre)	I should/would have been (Ich würde gewesen sein/Ich wäre gewesen)
I had had (Ich hatte gehabt)	I had (Ich hatte)	I should/would have (Ich würde haben/Ich hätte)	I should/would have had (Ich würde gehabt haben/Ich hätte gehabt)
I had got (Ich hatte bekommen)	I got (Ich bekam)	I should/would get (Ich würde bekommen/Ich bekäme)	I should/would have got (Ich würde bekommen haben/Ich hätte bekommen)

The combination of these four tenses can be illustrated with Hemingway's story:

Drevitts *had seen* what Boyle *had done*.
He *got* frightened.
He said there *would be* trouble.
He *would* not *have said* this if he had known Boyle's answer before.

5) Use, for instance, **direct speech** in a climactic story to point to important events towards the end. In other words, change from **summary or panoramic presentation** (raffende Darstellung) at the beginning to **scenic presentation** (szenisch dehnende Darstellung) at the end. Use the tenses of the **present tense group** in direct speech when the text form demands this.

...A heckler shouted (past tense),
"*Does* your mother *know* (present tense) *you're* out?" And the young politician said (past tense), ...

The present tense group

Present perfect	**Present**	**Will-future**	**Future perfect**
I have been (Ich bin gewesen)	I am (Ich bin)	I shall/will be (Ich werde sein)	I shall/will have been (Ich werde gewesen sein)
I have had (Ich habe gehabt)	I have (Ich habe)	I shall/will have (Ich werde haben)	I shall/will have had (Ich werde gehabt haben)
I have known (Ich habe gewußt)	I know (Ich weiß)	I shall/will know (Ich werde wissen)	I shall/will have known (Ich werde gewußt haben)

The combination of these four tenses can be illustrated with the heckler story:

The young politician said:
a) "I *have wanted* to talk to you for a long time."
b) "I *know* there *are* some people who *do not want* to listen to what I *have* to tell you."
c) "I *will be* brief in tonight's talk.
d) "If I talk too long, you *will have gone* to sleep by the end of my speech."

(CF. "TEXT FORM DICTIONARY", III, 2.)

Some areas of use

The shorter forms of stories are often told:
a) to illustrate a point or argument in a **comment** (CF. II, 10). The story then serves as the writer's **evidence** (Beweis[material]) from experience. The comment might, for example, begin like this:

In my view, the character Boyle in Hemingway's story should not be praised but strongly condemned for his way of acting.

This opening statement could then be followed by a **linking introduction** for the story:

Just consider what happened.

Then comes the **story** as evidence:

When the police car arrived, the two Hungarians had just left the cigar store. One man had got into the driver's seat, the other into the pickup box. When Boyle shot, they were backing their pickup out of the alley. They had started their car before the policemen arrived on the scene.

This, then, would be the **conclusion** to the comment:

So it is obvious that the Hungarians were not trying to evade arrest by speeding away.

b) to explain an aspect of a **text interpretation** (CF. II, 9) by speaking of what happened at some stage in **history.** The text interpretation could begin like this:

> The policemen's behaviour in the outlined situation shows that justice was crude in their town. What kind of town would we have to imagine?

This opening observation might then be followed by a **linking introduction** for the story:

> A brief look at the author's life may throw some light on this situation.

Now follows the **story:**

> The sketch "At two o'clock in the morning" was written in 1917/18. At that time Hemingway worked as a young reporter for the "Star" in Kansas City. Carlos Baker, who wrote Hemingway's life story, tells us that Kansas City was, at that time, a big city of 300,000 inhabitants. Only twenty years before, it had still been a noisy frontier town.

After this illustration, the **text interpretation** might be continued like this:

> This historical situation helps to explain why Boyle does not care very much about observing the law himself...

c) to illustrate general historical developments by telling the reader about certain personal experiences. The following is a **personal story** told by a former Mexican migrant worker in the U.S. She wants to show how the small California farmer's work and attitude differs from the big growers':

> *I told* this grower we had families interested in buying some of his land. He didn't let me go any further. He asked me if we had half a million dollars. [Laughs.] He was paying us seventy-five cents an hour, picking cotton and cantaloupes (Melonenart) for him for nine, ten years...
> A friend of ours said: "I'll rent you six acres." We *started* farming those six acres. We were out there *from morning till late,* on our hands and knees, planting tomatoes. *There was* the risk of a cold wave *coming* and killing our plants...
> *One day* we had *finished* planting and said: "*Tomorrow* we'll put the hot caps on." They're cap-shaped papers with wire. *Around two or three o'clock* I heard on the radio – I always carry a little portable – I heard the weather *was gonna be* twenty-three degrees (– 5° Celsius). It *was gonna kill* our plants. I was scared. I ran back to the group and said: "Hey, it's gonna freeze tonight, we're gonna lose our plants." *Right away* we *started* putting the hot caps on.
> We put dirt around it to hold it down. We had them by the thousands. It was very windy and very cold. We *started* out there on our hands and knees. I was crying. It was beautiful. I'm not calling it beautiful, my crying. But to have little children five, six years old helping us, because they knew how important it was to save those plants. The wind was very strong, it was just ripping those paper caps off of our hands, and

you could see them rolling. [Laughs.] We ran out of caps. Okay, each of us got a hoe (Hacke) and *started* pulling dirt over our plants, very gently. We covered all of them. We came home, *it was dark*, cold, and wet.

The next morning we were all anxious to find out what had happened *during the night*. Oh, it was great to go out there and remove the dirt from those plants and watch 'em shoot straight up like anything. We saved every one of 'em. It took hard work to do it.

If it had been one of the big growers, what would have happened? The farmer would just go out there and look and see all the dead plants, and he'd say: "Oh, what the heck"... He would get on his pickup, push a button, lift up a telephone, and call the nursery to bring over this certain amount of thousands of plants and call the workers to plant them over again. That's his way of farming.

(STUDS TERKEL, *AMERICAN DREAMS: LOST AND FOUND*, LONDON, 1985 (1980), PP. 196–8)

3. Reports

Definition: In a report (Bericht), we tell others about past actions and events as facts that can be checked as true. We use an objective point of view. In contrast to stories, we therefore make exact and correct references to time, place and persons in reports. We usually start from an exact time reference, such as a date or the time of the clock. Common variants of this text form are the biographical note, the news story, and historical accounts generally.

What all forms of reports have in common with stories is that we use them to speak about what happened in time.

Forms

The following short texts illustrate how we write short reports such as biographical notes, news stories, and historical accounts.

a) A **biographical note.** The most important dates of a person's life are given to create a **chronological order:**

▭ William Golding was born at St. Columb Minor, Cornwall, *in 1911*, and educated at Marlborough Grammar School and Brasenose College, Oxford. ▤ He joined the Navy *in 1940* and served in cruisers, destroyers, minesweepers, and a rocket ship which he commanded *at the end of the war*. He saw action against submarines, aircraft, and the Bismarck, and was present *at the "D-Day" landings*, and the attack on Walcheren. *In 1945* he be-

▭ Beginning
a) A situation: exact references to time (dates), place (names of places, countries, etc.), persons (their real Christian names and surnames), and actions in the past

▤ Middle
b) Exact time adverbials to form a clear chronological order
c) Use of a neutral style; no personal impressions or opinions

came a schoolmaster at Bishop Wordsworth's School, Salisbury, where he remained *until 1961.* ⬓ *In 1962,* he was resident writer at Hollins College, Virginia.

(WILLIAM GOLDING, *LORD OF THE FLIES*. HARMONDSWORTH, 1963, P. 1)

⬓ End
d) The last date in the sequence (here: "In 1962")

2) A **news story.** To create interest, the chronological order is reversed (umgekehrt). The reader is given first what came last in time. In other words, he is shown the **effects** of actions so that he may become interested in the **causes:**

⬒ **Baby taken as mother shops**
Police in cars with loudspeakers toured Burton-on-Trent, Staffs, yesterday appealing for information *after* a three-month-old baby had been snatched from her pram.

⬒ Beginning
a) A situation: the exact time, place, people's names, and actions in the past
b) The last action comes first (i.e. as an *effect*)
c) The action that came first in time comes at the end of the introductory paragraph (i.e. as the *cause* of b)

⊟ Cathy Whetton had been left outside a High Street supermarket *while* her mother, Mrs Lynette Whetton, 23, of All Saints Road, did her shopping. *When* the mother returned the pram had disappeared and *later* it was found empty 150 yards away. Police checked cars and buses and alerted neighbouring police forces.

⊟ Middle
d) Use of time clauses to form a chronological order in individual paragraphs (here: "after", "while", "when")

A spokesman for the supermarket said: "Many mothers leave children in prams and pushchairs in the covered precinct outside the shop and nobody ever thinks that something awful like this could happen."

e) The less important details or events come in paragraphs towards the end

⬓ Mrs Whetton and her husband, Kenneth, have two other daughters – Fay, seven, and Vicky, 21 months – who went into the shop with her.

(*THE OBSERVER*, 5 NOV. 1972)

⬓ End
f) The least important detail of information comes at the end of the news story

3) A **historical account** from a reference book (Nachschlagewerk) on world events:

⬒ In a dramatic turn of events Rajiv Gandhi became prime minister of India after his mother, Indira Gandhi, was gunned down by Sikhs on her own personal bodyguard team *on Oct. 31, 1984*

⬒ Beginning
a) The narrated situation: the exact time, place, names, and actions in the past

[...] ⊟ The assassination, generally considered to be retribution (Vergeltung) for her June 1984 order for government troops to storm the Golden Temple in Amritsar, the Sikhs' most holy shrine, touched off a major political crisis as well as large-scale violence by Hindus, who randomly (wahllos) murdered more than 1,000 Sikhs.

As one of his first official acts as prime minister, Gandhi appealed for peace in a radio broadcast saying, "Nothing would hurt the soul of our beloved Indira Gandhi more than the occurrence of violence in any part of the country." *One day after* the official 12-day mourning (Trauer-) period, Gandhi was unanimously (einstimmig) named *(November 12)* president of the Congress (I) party, and *on the following day* he called for parliamentary elections *on December 24*. ⊡ Those elections returned him to power in a landslide (überwältigender Sieg) dwarfing (in den Schatten stellen) any experienced by his mother or his grandfather.

(*1985 Britannica Book of the Year*, Chicago, 1985, p.97)

⊟ Middle

b) Use of verbs of action in the past tense (here: "touched off", "murdered", etc.)

c) Use of exact time adverbials, so that a chronological order is formed

⊡ End

d) The last action or event in the narrated chronological order

General steps for writing a report

1) Use an introduction in which you refer to a **situation** in the past. Refer exactly and truthfully to time, place, persons, and a first action or event (when? where? who? what?).

In a dramatic turn of events Rajiv Gandhi *(person)* became prime minister *(event)* of India *(place)* after his mother, Indira Gandhi, was gunned down *(first action)* by Sikhs on her own bodyguard team on Oct. 31, 1984 *(time)*.

*

2) Move on from your opening time expression by using further **time words** in your text so that you create a **chronological order** of dates. You can use:

a) a simple sequence ([Ab-]Folge) of **verbs in the past tense.** For instance: "...the following day he *called* for parliamentary elections on December 24. Those elections *returned* him to power..."

b) simple **time adverbs** for short jumps in time: "When the mother returned the pram had disappeared *and later* it was found empty 150 yards away."
c) exact and verifiable (überprüfbar) **time adverbials:** "*One day after* the official 12-day mourning period, Gandhi was unanimously named *(November 12)* president..."
d) **time clauses** with "when", "while", "as soon as", "after", "before", "until", etc. For instance: "Cathy Whetton had been left outside a High Street supermarket *while her mother, Mrs Lynette Whetton, of All Saints Road, did her shopping. When the mother returned* the pram had disappeared..."

3) Use the tenses of the **past tense group** in most narrative text forms: the past perfect, past tense, conditional I, and conditional II (cf. II, 2, "General steps", [4]).

4) Use **direct speech** to mention the most important speech events in your report. In the quoted speech, you can also use subjective comments, interpretations, or any other text form. Use the tenses of the present tense group in direct speech when the text form demands (erfordern) this (cf. II, 2, "General steps", [5]). Use the past tense group when the quoted speaker tells a story.
(cf. "Text form dictionary", III, 3.)

Some areas of use

The shorter forms of reports are often presented:
a) to report **historical events,** such as chapters from a public figure's life, or from a people's or nation's history:

> There are not many records of how and when North America was filled with people. The earliest cultures can only generally be defined as hunting and gathering communities. These ancestors (Vorfahren) of the native Americans originally came from Asia. They began crossing from Asia into Alaska about thirty or forty thousand years ago, using the thousand-mile wide land bridge that appeared when the oceans fell some 300 feet during the Ice Age. They came in a series of migrations, perhaps following herds eastward whenever the Bering Sea sank and the land mass rose. The last great wave of settlers reached America about eight thousand years ago. By that time, those who had come before, were spreading to the east and south from Alaska. Some 25,000 years after their invasion began, they had taken possession of all of North and South America.

b) to explain an aspect of a **text interpretation** (cf. II, 9) by reporting what exactly happened in history. For instance, the following text on poverty in the U.S. may have to be interpreted:

> "...and now there is that second issue (Frage, Problem) to trouble policy-makers as well: Could it be that social programs actually have made poverty attractive? On one side of the debate are arrayed (aufstellen) followers of a liberal tradition that began with Franklin D. Roosevelt's New Deal..." (cf. *Los Angeles Times,* July 29, 1985)

The assignment (Aufgabe) for your text interpretation may read:

> "How might one characterize the philosophy behind programs such as 'Franklin D. Roosevelt's New Deal'?"

Your text interpretation may **begin** like this:

> The philosophy behind programs such as "Franklin D. Roosevelt's New Deal" was that the poor, especially the unemployed, were not a private, but a national responsibility (Verantwortlichkeit). Roosevelt's New Deal legislation between 1933 and 1939 put an end to the traditional U.S. economic philosophy of laissez-faire (Gewährenlassen), which gave unfair advantage (Vorteil) to the ruthless entrepreneur (rücksichtsloser Unternehmer). The New Deal legislation introduced principles of a planned economy aimed at balancing the conflicting interests of employers and employees.

At this point, you may want to give a detailed **historical report:**

> Among the most important long-term social reforms introduced *during the New Deal period* were the Social Security Act *(1935)*, which, for the first time in U.S. history, introduced unemployment compensation (Arbeitslosenunterstützung), old-age and widows' pensions, and disability insurance (Invalidenversicherung); the National Labor Relations Act (the Wagner Act, *1935*), which guaranteed workers the right of collective bargaining (Tarifverhandlungen) through unions; and the Fair Labor Standards Act *(1938)*, which fixed maximum working hours (at 40 per week) and provided for minimum wages. Simultaneously, it outlawed child labour in certain industries.

In the **conclusion,** you will return to the text interpretation:

> Legislative measures such as Roosevelt's New Deal have acknowledged (anerkennen) that social programs are not a question of self-reliance (Eigenverantwortung) or individual acts of charity (Barmherzigkeit), but a responsibility of public administration.

Expository text forms

In expository ([ek'spɒzɪtrɪ], erklärend) texts we try to analyse (['ænəlaɪz], zerlegen [in Bestandteile]) and explain a general idea or concept (gedankliche Vorstellung). **Definitions** in the shorter dictionaries, longer **explications** (Erläuterungen) in large reference books (Nachschlagewerke), **outlines, summaries** and **text interpretations** can all be grouped as expository text forms or variants of them.
All expository text forms deal with how we u n d e r s t a n d what a word, a term (Begriff), or a text means. They are connected with c o m p r e h e n s i o n (Verstehen, Begreifen) through the formation of concepts.

4. Definitions

Definition: In a definition, we explain what an ordinary word or a particular term means. In everyday situations, we often simply use more familiar ([fəˈmɪljə], bekannt, vertraut) words, such as synonyms or antonyms, to define a term (for instance, when we say that a "fable" is a kind of story).
In a more detailed definition, however, we usually define a term according to two or three areas, using familiar words:
1) we refer to the larger group or class of things that the term refers to. We use a more **inclusive term** (such as "story", which includes a fable);
2) we use familiar words to refer to a number of particular elements as **characteristics** that distinguish (unterscheiden) our term from other similar terms in its class (for instance, by saying that a fable is a kind of story *in which animals behave like human beings*);
3) we often also use an **example** to illustrate the more general definition we have given. We can say, for instance, that James Thurber's "The Very Proper Gander" is a fable in which *a family of geese is driven from a farmyard by a group of chickens who dislike the father goose and call him a traitor*.
The aim of a definition is to make it possible for others to form a clear mental (geistig) picture, a c o n c e p t , in connection with a word or expression that we use.

Forms

Generally, we can distinguish between different kinds of short definition and the long definition. Short definitions are the most frequent forms: the very short one that uses only more familiar synonyms or antonyms; the one in which we give the class that the term refers to and a number of characteristics (the class-plus-characteristics definition); and the short definition in which we also add an example.

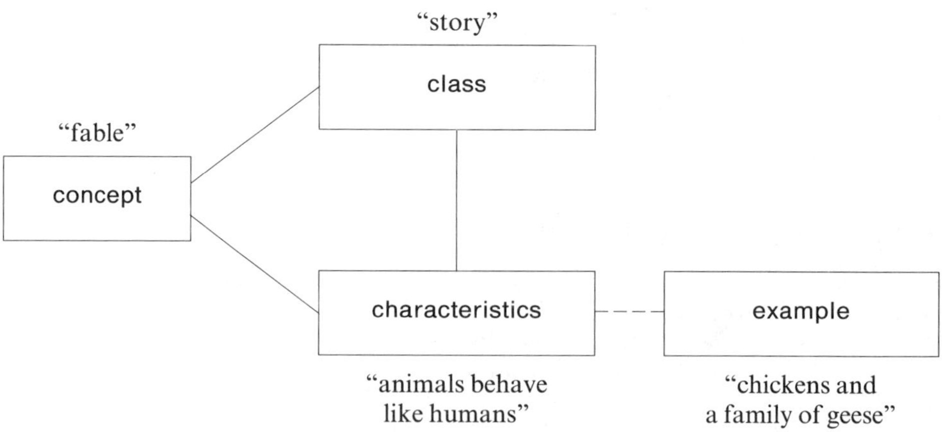

1) Very **short definitions** using more familiar synonyms or antonyms:

"X" means roughly the same as "Y".
"X" is almost synonymous [sɪˈnɒnɪməs] with "Y".
"X" is a near synonym of "Y".
"X" is roughly the opposite of "Y".
"X" is opposite in meaning to "Y".
"X" is (roughly) the antonym of "Y".
"X" and "Y" are antonymous [ænˈtɒnɪməs] terms.

2) The short **class-plus-characteristics definition** (without an example):

A "dictionary" is *a book* which lists [1] the words of a language [2] alphabetically [3] and gives their meanings [4], pronunciations [5], and various information about their use [6].

a) Use of an inclusive class term (here: "a book")
b) Use of familiar words to refer to distinctive features (see 1, 2, 3, etc., which characterise a "dictionary")

3) The short **class-plus-characteristics definition** with an **example:**

By "slang" we mean a kind of *language* that is used among friends or acquaintances (Bekannte). Slang is considered very informal or not polite with strangers. Often, slang words are vivid (anschaulich) words that were once used and understood only by particular groups of people. "Dough" was originally used by bakers for the mixture of flour (Mehl) and water to make bread. It became a slang word in the United States for money. In this new sense, the slang word is used and understood by most Americans. After some time, however, slang words are replaced by newer ones.

a) Use of an inclusive class term (here: "a kind of language")
b) Use of familiar words to refer to distinctive features
c) An example to illustrate the more general definition (here: "Dough")

4) In **long definitions,** a word may also be explained by the meaning or meanings that it once had in the past. Moreover, the elements of which the word is composed may be explained. Particular research (Forschung) is often needed to find out about the past meanings and origin of a word.

General steps for writing a definition

1) Place the term that you want to define in a larger **class** of things with which it can be linked. Use an **inclusive term.** Questions such as the following can help you: What kind of thing is "X"? What kind of idea is "X"?

> By "slang" we mean a kind of *language*.

2) List the specific **characteristics** by which your term "X" is different from the other objects or ideas of the larger class. Give the **distinctive features**. The following questions can help you: What does "X" consist of? What is "X" used for?

> By "slang" we mean a kind of *language* that is used among friends or acquaintances. Slang is considered very informal or not polite with strangers. ...

3) Think of an **example** for illustration that can be easily understood by most people. Take your example from an area of experience (Erfahrungsbereich) which the people for whom you are writing your definition are familiar with.

> ..."Dough" [, for instance,] was originally used by bakers for the mixture of flour and water to make bread. It became a slang word in the United States for money.

4) Try to be precise and objective in your definition. Definitions in which a speaker deliberately distorts (absichtlich verzerren) the meaning of a word or expression are characteristic only of text forms of subjective persuasion (Überredung), such as a comment or a piece of propaganda.
The following short, deliberately distorting definition may be used as part of a comment:

> ... But "leisure" (a hateful word which I understand to mean a form of docile idleness [leicht zu lenkendes Nichtstun] in which much money is both invested and spent) is something of such overriding (äußerst) importance that nobody [...] thinking about new technology can afford to ignore it.
>
> (MICHAEL BYWATER, "EDUCATION'S BLIND SPOT ABOUT HUMAN PROGRESS", IN: *THE OBSERVER*, 6 OCTOBER 1985)

5) When you use a short definition within a longer text – for instance, in a text interpretation (CF. II, 9) or in a comment (CF. II, 10) – you will normally introduce it by **expressions for announcing a definition.** Your reader or listener will then know what different text form or information to expect within the larger text.
In the following text, a short definition is announced as part of a comment:

> ... before we think [...] of the notion (Vorstellung) that technology precipitates (beschleunigen) unemployment, I want to state the obvious fact that, when we talk about jobs and employment, we are really using Humpty-Dumpty *definitions* whereby words mean what we want them to mean. *The first* and most pernicious (schädlich) *of these definitions is that* a job is what someone else gives you.
>
> (MICHAEL BYWATER, *LOC. CIT.*)

(CF. "TEXT FORM DICTIONARY", III, 4.)

Some areas of use

Short definitions, with or without examples, are often used:
a) in a **longer piece of speech or writing** to explain words and expressions which the listeners or readers need to understand correctly or more precisely in order to follow what we are saying. The writer may, for instance, start with the **distinctive features:**

> Air is moving (that is, winds are blowing) at both high and low levels in the atmosphere. The high level winds, blowing at ten miles or more up, are those met by air liners. At this height they say they are flying "above the weather", because it is the low level winds, much nearer the earth's surface, which are concerned with our weather.

Then he will introduce the defined **new term:**

> A wind which blows steadily always in the same direction is called a *prevailing wind.*

He may also add an **example:**

> In the days of sailing ships certain of these prevailing winds which blew across the oceans were used by ships and were known as *"trade winds"*.
>
> (FROM: F. E. NEWING AND RICHARD BOWOOD, *THE LADYBIRD BOOK OF THE WEATHER.* LOUGHBOROUGH, 1962, P. 12)

b) as part of a **text interpretation** (CF. II, 6) to enable others (es anderen zu ermöglichen) to understand the **technical terms** we use as the guiding concepts in our reading of a text. The text interpretation may begin like this:

> Talking about the animals and their behaviour in Thurber's fable "The owl who was God", we may, for instance, use a concept of text interpretation such as "role".

This may be followed by the insertion (Einschub) of a **short definition** (class plus characteristics and example):

> The term "role" can here be defined simply as the ways of behaviour which an individual learns in the society (Gesellschaft) in which he grows up. He or she chooses different ways of behaving (or, different roles) in different social situations. For instance, someone will take a different role in the family than in his or her work place or as a customer in a public office.

Then the **text interpretation** might continue like this:

> In Thurber's fable the role of the red fox can be explained as a specific kind of behaviour in a political community. He distinguishes himself from the others by...

c) as part of a line of argumentation, for instance, in a **comment** (CF. II, 10) that is part of a political speech:

> I here define "socialism" / "capitalism" as...

5. Explications

Definition: In an explication (Erläuterung, [genaue] Erklärung), we systematically explain and classify (klassifizieren) a general thought content. We usually start from a general concept (allgemeine begriffliche Vorstellung) and systematically analyse (zerlegen) it into its more particular elements. We then show how these elements are connected with each other, and in this way create an analytical order (eine in Elemente zerlegende Ordnung, Folge).
If we think of concepts such as "literature", "communication", "socialism", or "imperialism", we can see the difference between a definition (cf. II, 4) and an explication. Such comprehensive (umfassend) concepts cannot be explained and understood fully by a short definition alone. Even a long definition could not explain in detail the matter (Sache, Gegenstand). It would concentrate only on the *words* "literature", "communication", etc., as elements of the language.
In explications, we speak from the point of view of an objective expert who tries to give a less informed reader some clearer idea of a special field of knowledge (Wissensgebiet). As an expository text form, explication is connected with comprehension (Verstehen, Begreifen). Explications enable us to form concepts.

Forms

The following text on the concept of "literature" can illustrate how a short definition is continued with an explication in an **analytical order:**

["Literature" sometimes] means anything written, as in "Please send me literature on breeding (züchten) guppies (Millionenfisch, Guppie)." Most critics regard *such a definition* as too broad because it includes pamphlets on how to make money from guppies, and too narrow because it excludes such oral (mündlich) compositions as ballads and folk tales (Volksmärchen).

Beginning
a) A short definition of the term to introduce the general concept

Perhaps one can *begin by saying* that literature uses language in compositions that are valuable in themselves. A pamphlet on breeding guppies is valuable chiefly as a guide to breeding guppies; a short story about a man who breeds guppies is valuable (if it has values) chiefly in itself. *Furthermore*, this story – or poem or play – is recognized as a fiction (Erfindung des Geistes); it is not historical, but imaginative, and the reader finds this ficti-

Middle
b) Elements or aspects of the concept (here: "uses language in compositions that are valuable in themselves")
c) Use of an opening signal to show the beginning of the analysis, i.e. an initiator (here: "begin by saying")
d) Use of additive signals for each new element to show the analytical order (here: "furthermore")
e) Use of examples that can help to explain a particular element of the concept (here: "may")
f) Use of signals that point to an explanation by an example (explicatory [erklärend] signals; here: "just as")

tious (erdacht) man and his world interesting. The story *may* begin by claiming to be historical, *and it may* be set in a real city (Dublin) during a recognizable (erkennbar) era (early twentieth century); but it is nevertheless accepted by the reader as a fiction, *just as* the spectator at a play accepts the scene in front of him as a fiction, although it too is set in Dublin.

❐ There is, *in short,* an element of make-believe (Schein). The poet may say (as Tennyson says in "In Memoriam"), "Dark house, by which once more I stand." Perhaps Tennyson did stand by the house as he wrote the lines, but probably he didn't. In any case (wie auch immer), though he seems to address the house, it is the reader, not the house, who is in fact listening.

❐ End (of one section)
g) Use of signals that point to a result, summary or shorter reformulation (Umformulierung)

In addition to this element of make-believe, there is in literature (as opposed to other compositions of words) considerable importance in the arrangements of sound and in the richness of suggestion. In fact, richness of suggestion is often said to distinguish poetry and verse...

h) Use of another additive signal to show the analytical order

(S. BARNET ET AL., *A DICTIONARY OF LITERARY TERMS.* LONDON, 1964, PP. 87–8)

General steps for writing an explication

1) Use an introduction with a **general concept** as a topic for analysis.

What do we understand by "literature"? Perhaps one can begin by saying that literature uses language in compositions that are valuable in themselves...

2) Think of different ways of understanding, or of **elements** and aspects of the concept, so that the whole (das Ganze) can be seen in its particular parts.

literature:
- is recognized as a fiction
- uses language in compositions that are valuable in themselves
- places particular importance on the arrangements of sound and on the richness of suggestion
- ...

*

3) Place the listed elements in a systematic **order** that can best show how these elements fit together (zusammenpassen) and how they form a meaningful whole. You can start with those elements that are the most general ones, or the easiest ones to understand, and end with the more particular elements or those more difficult to understand. You can then turn your first **list** of elements (see [2] above) into a re-ordered and **numbered topic outline** (CF. II, 6).

literature:
1. uses language in compositions that are valuable in themselves
2. is recognized as a fiction
3. places particular importance on the arrangements of sound and on the richness of suggestion

4) In your text, use opening expressions for each of your numbered subtopics (Unterthemen) which tell the reader when you are adding another aspect **(additive signals)** or that you are explaining another aspect **(explicatory signals).** Use an expression to show the beginning of your analytical order (an **initiator** [Anfangssignal]).
For the first subtopic, your text could read like this:

Perhaps one *can begin by saying* [initiator] that literature uses language in compositions that are valuable in themselves...

The second subtopic can be announced in this way:

Furthermore, this story – or poem or play – is recognized as a fiction...
The story *may [, for instance,]* begin by claiming to be historical, and it *may [, for instance,]* be set in a real city...
...it is nevertheless accepted by the reader as a fiction, *just as [, for example,]* the spectator at a play accepts the scene in front of him as a fiction...

The third subtopic could have the following signal:

In addition to this element of make-believe, there is in literature (as opposed to other compositions of words) considerable importance in the arrangements of sound and in the richness of suggestion...

5) Illustrate your subtopics by **examples** that can help you to explain a particular element of your concept.

There is, in short, an element of make-believe. The poet *may [, for instance,]* say (*as Tennyson says in* "In Memoriam"), "Dark house..."

6) To support your analytical order, you may repeat the topical keywords (thematische Schlüsselwörter) after longer text divisions in between. These **long-distance signals** (Fernsignale) in the text can help the reader to remember the aspects you have already mentioned some time before.
The end of the second subtopic could read like this:

...There is, in short, *an element of make-believe.* The poet may say...

Later, before the third subtopic is mentioned, that keyword may be repeated:

> In addition to *this element of make-believe,* there is in literature [...] considerable importance in the arrangements of sound and in the richness of suggestion...

7) Write your explications from an objective point of view. Use a factual (sachlich), **neutral style.** As you write, explain all the technical terms that your readers will probably (wahrscheinlich) not be familiar with.

> [see the second subtopic when the writer introduces the technical term "fiction":]
> Furthermore, this story [...] is recognized as *a fiction;* it is *not historical,* but *imaginative,* and the reader finds *this fictitious* man and his world interesting...

*

8) Sum up your **results** after a number of paragraphs and again at the end of your explication.

> [see the end of the second subtopic:]
> ...There is, *in short,* an element of make-believe.

(Cf. "Text form dictionary", III, 5.)

Some areas of use

Explications are often used:
a) as important parts of **text interpretations** (cf. II, 9) to explain and illustrate certain concepts, especially those which the text refers to only indirectly:
The **introduction** to a paragraph of text interpretation may read like this.

> Drevitts's choice of words in his comment [on Boyle in Hemingway's "At two o'clock in the morning"; cf. II, 2] clearly indicates that he thinks they will be held responsible and perhaps even be charged (anklagen) with the killings.

Then an illustration with an **explication** may follow. It starts from the elements of a concept and then names it at the end:

> When he says, "you oughtn't to have done it" (l. ...), his choice of the auxiliary emphasizes a moral obligation. *Similarly,* when he says, "There's liable to be a hell of a lot of trouble", the semi-auxiliary "be liable to" indicates that he knows these killings cannot easily be justified before their superiors (Vorgesetzte). In these reactions, Drevitts can be seen to differ markedly (['mɑ:kɪdlɪ], deutlich) from his companion. He knows and feels obliged to *the law of the country* as regards the protection of a citizen's life. He speaks from *a sense of justice.* (cf. II, 2 for Hemingway's text)

b) as independent **research papers** (wissenschaftliche Abhandlungen, Referate) or **treatises** (['tri:tɪsɪz], [lange] Abhandlungen), usually as contributions to a book or independent publication, such as a scholarly journal (wissenschaftliche Zeitschrift).
c) as **long articles** in reference books (Nachschlagewerke) and encyclopaedias ([en,saɪkləʊ'pi:djəz]). In these, passages of explication are usually combined with definitions (cf. II, 4), reports (cf. II, 3), comments (cf. II, 10), or even technical descriptions (cf. II, 1).

6. Outlines

Definition: An outline (Gliederung) shows how the main ideas (Hauptgedanken) or topics (Themen) of a text have been arranged. We can say that a topic outline presents the compositional plan (Plan für den Aufbau, Entwurf) of a text.
We use a topic outline to show at a glance (auf einen Blick) or to explain how we have ordered the main ideas for a longer text. Each of the listed topics can later be used in our text as a heading (Überschrift) or a subheading (Untertitel, -überschrift).
Like the definition (CF. II, 4) and the explication (CF. II, 5), a topic outline has an analytical order. This order can easily be understood because it is normally further supported by a listing order (aufzählende, auflistende Ordnung) using numerals (or letters of the alphabet).
An outline is an expository text form. It is connected with comprehension (Verstehen, Begreifen).

Forms

1) A **topic outline** (Stichwortgliederung) to point to the topics of a text that follows. It is also known as a **word outline** because it does not use complete sentences, but only short captions (Titel, Überschriften):

North American Peoples and Cultures

1. The people
   1.1 Physical types
   1.2 Population and languages
   1.3 Culture areas
2. Prehistory
   2.1 Early cultures
   2.2 The archaic cultures
   2.3 Early agriculturalists
   2.4 Mississippi Valley and peripheral woodlands
   2.5 Southwestern village farmers
3. Evolution of contemporary North American Indians
   3.1 Colonial policies
   3.2 United States policy

(ADAPTED FROM: *ENCYCLOPAEDIA BRITANNICA*, 1975, VOL. 13)

a) Analysis of the general topic into a number of more particular elements (see "The people", "Prehistory", etc.)
b) The elements, listed in some convincing analytical order. Use of numerals (Zahlwörter) to show the subdivisions (Untergliederungen)
c) Use of words as topics and subtopics which can again be analysed into elements (here: "Prehistory" into "Early cultures", "The Archaic cultures", etc.)
d) Use of parallel construction (here: only noun groups "The people", "Prehistory", etc.)

2) A **sentence outline** to give a short survey (Überblick) of the topics:

North American Peoples and Cultures

1. *The people* of North America can be characterized
   1.1 by the basic *physical types* they represent,
   1.2 by counts of the *population* and differences between their *languages,* and
   1.3 by a limited number of *culture areas* for groups of tribes.

a) Subtopics, made dependent (abhängig) on one verb (here: "*characterized* by", etc.) for parallel construction

2. The *prehistory* of these people can be subdivided into
   2.1 *early cultures,*
   2.2 the *archaic cultures,*
   [...]

b) Use of numerals for a listing order within each sentence for the subdivisions (here: "2.1", "2.2", etc.)

3. The *evolution of contemporary North American Indians* is closely connected with
   3.1 *colonial policies,*
   3.2 *United States policy.*

General steps for writing an outline

1) Think of your topic (for instance, "North American Peoples and Cultures") as an expression that refers to or classifies (nach Klassen einteilen) different aspects or elements. Take your topic as a collective term (Sammelbegriff) and **list the elements** that go into it as they come to your mind, in no fixed order.

North American peoples and cultures

- Who was there before recorded history began – prehistory?
-- earliest cultures, later cultures – the population
- policies that the Europeans pursued (verfolgen) towards Indians
-- policies in colonial times (up to about 1780/90)
-- policies of the new United States up to today (1780/90 onwards)
- characterization of Indians as an ethnic group (Volksgruppe)
-- types of face and build (Körperbau), language, cultural traditions

a) No need to use parallel construction (here: noun groups are mixed with a complete sentence)
b) Use of signals for possible subtopics (here: "––")

2) Now give your first list (see [1] above) some convincing **order.** Think of changes from the past to the present; of a progression (Übergang, Fortschreiten) from particular to general aspects, etc.
A change from the distant past to modern times and the present might give the following order:

- Who was there before recorded history began → prehistory?
- Policies that the Europeans pursued towards Indians

A progression from particular to more and more general aspects may lead to this order:

-- types of face and build (physical types)
-- population
-- languages
-- culture areas

3) Use numerals (['nju:mərəlz], Zahlwörter) to support a convincing **analytical order** in your ordered list, and distinguish (unterscheiden) between main topics and subtopics (Unterthemen). A topic which is subdivided must have at least two subtopics.

2 Prehistory
3 Policies that the Europeans pursued towards Indians (Evolution of present-day Indians)
1 The people
1.1 Physical types
1.2 Population and languages
[...]

4) Use the same numerals, topics and subtopics as **headings** and **subheadings** in your longer texts. In technical terms, support your analytic order by a **listing order** in your longer texts. Use a separate line for each heading.

[...]
2. Prehistory
There are not many records (Aufzeichnungen) of how North America was peopled (bevölkern). The earliest settlers can only be generally defined as hunting and gathering people (Jäger und Sammler) [...]
2.1 Early cultures. The earliest distinct traditions in North America can be placed at about 10,000 to 8,000 B. C. One tradition is that of the big-game (Großwild) hunters of the West, the Great Plains, and eastern North America [...]

(Cf. "Text form dictionary", III, 6.)

Some areas of use

Topic outlines are used:
a) as **preliminary surveys** (einleitende Überblicke) of longer talks on a subject, especially those in which explication and argumentation or narration are mixed:

> In my report on the North American peoples and cultures, *I shall deal with three main aspects. First* I shall characterize the people – the basic physical type they represent, their numbers and languages, and the main culture areas in which groups of tribes are to be found. *In a second step* I shall look at the earliest people in North America, the prehistory of North American Indians...

b) as a **survey of the results** of a speech, discussion, or interpretive ([ɪn'tɜ:prətɪv]) discourse (Interpretationsgespräch) on a text:

> In our discussion of Hemingway's story "At two o'clock in the morning", the following topics were dealt with:
> 1. The policemen's encounter with the two Hungarians
> 2. Boyle's way of acting
> 3. Drevitts's behaviour
> 4. Boyle's reaction to Drevitts
> 5. The conclusion to the story

As a so-called **agenda,** a topic outline usually introduces the minutes (Protokolle) of more or less public meetings (CF. II, 8 ON SUMMARIZING MINUTES).

c) as **notes,** the result of one's reading and subdivision (Untergliederung) of a longer text according to its main ideas or topics. Such a topic outline can serve as the basis of a coherent ([kəʊ'hɪərənt], zusammenhängend) summary (CF. II, 7).
A topic outline of Hemingway's "Old Man at the Bridge" might read like this:

1. The situation at a bridge in Spain: many people are fleeing across it, except an old man (see lines ... – ...)
2. The conversation between the I-narrator and the old man: after exploring the dangerous situation at the bridgehead, he tries to persuade the old man to move along with the other people (see lines ... – ...)
3. The narrator's view of the general war situation and the old man's probable fate (wahrscheinliches Schicksal) (see lines ... – ...)

d) to give the writer of a long text a clear **guideline** and direction during the writing process. The usefulness of a topic outline can be greatly increased when the writer repeats the numbered topics as **headings** and **subheadings** later in the body of his text. Note that the headings or titles used in newspaper articles are commonly called **headlines.** They often differ from the headings of other kinds of publication.

7. Summaries

Definition: In a summary (Inhaltsangabe, Zusammenfassung) we present the information of a much longer text in much shorter reading or listening time. Through a summary we can inform others about the contents of, for instance, a book or a long chapter (Kapitel) in the length of only one short paragraph (thematisch geschlossener Kurzabschnitt, Paragraph) or even (sogar) of only one sentence. The original text is translated into a new text.
A summary can be based on a topic outline (CF. II, 6) of the longer text. It can also start from concepts of text interpretation by which the topics of a long text can be easily ordered. A novel, for instance, can be summed up with the help of concepts such as setting in space (Schauplatz), setting in time (zeitliche Einbettung), characters, and plot (durch Gegensätze ausgelöste Ursache-Wirkungskette im Handlungsverlauf).
Its analytical order shows that the summary is an expository text form. It aims at (zielen auf) comprehension (Verstehen, Begreifen).

Forms

1) A one-sentence summary of a paragraph. We may, for instance, want to refer to the opening paragraph of Hemingway's "Old Man at the Bridge":

> An old man with steel rimmed spectacles and very dusty clothes sat by the side of the road. There was a pontoon bridge across the river and carts, trucks, and men, women and children were crossing it. The mule-drawn carts staggered up the steep bank from the bridge with soldiers helping push against the spokes of the wheels. The trucks ground up and away heading out of it all and the peasants plodded along in the ankle deep dust. But the old man sat there without moving. He was too tired to go any farther.

The **one-sentence summary,** then, could read like this:

> Many people are fleeing across a bridge, except an old man who remains sitting by the road after crossing the bridge.

a) Use of summary (zusammenfassend) expressions for several words of the original that are similar in meaning (see "people" and "fleeing")
b) No comment on or interpretation of the original text
c) Use of the present tense group

2) A one-paragraph summary of a short story of chapter length. It may be based on this topic outline:

Hemingway's "Old Man at the Bridge"
1. The situation at a bridge in Spain: many people are fleeing across it, except an old man (ll. ... – ...)
2. The conversation between the I-narrator and the old man: after exploring the dangerous situation at the bridgehead, the narrator tries to persuade the old man to move on with the other people (ll. ... – ...)
3. The narrator's view of the general war situation and the old man's probable fate (ll. ... – ...)

(For information on writing a topic outline, cf. II, 6.)

The **one-paragraph summary** might then take this form:

Hemingway's short story "Old Man at the Bridge" **introduces** the reader to a dangerous situation at a bridge. Many people are fleeing across it, except an old man. He remains sitting by the side of the road after crossing the bridge. The narrator passes and crosses to the other side of the bridge to explore the bridgehead beyond. On returning, he enters into *a conversation* with the old man. He tries to *persuade* him to move on with the other refugees. But the old man's *thoughts are with* the few animals he had to leave behind. He does not follow the officer's *advice*. **At the end,** the narrator assesses (bewerten) the general situation and what the old man's fate is likely to be.

a) Identification of the author and his publication (author's name, kind of text, title; if necessary: place, publisher, and year of publication)
b) Use of signals to point to the opening and closing divisions (Abschnitte) of the original text (here: "introduces", "At the end") (cf. I, "Rule 3")
c) Use of the tenses of the present group (cf. II, 2)
d) Summary of direct speech passages (dialogue) by summary expressions and monologue

3) A **one-paragraph summary** of a short story of chapter length, based on concepts of text interpretation for narration, will for instance use the concepts of setting in space, setting in time, action, and plot (CF. II, 2):

Hemingway's short story "Old Man at the Bridge" is *set in* Spain at *the time of* the Civil War from 1936–39. The *action is generated by* a soldier at a bridge across the river Ebro. He *tries* to make an old man move on to safety with other fugitives. The old man, however, is thinking only of the animals he had to leave behind. When the soldier realises that he has failed in his attempt (because *the old man will not or cannot* move on), he closes with *a comment* on the general situation in the war and the old man's probable fate in it.

a) Force 1 of the plot (here: the soldier tries to *cause* certain actions)

b) Force 2 of the plot (here: the old man reacts against the soldier's intentions; an *effect* produced by the soldier)
c) Use of other technical terms (Fachbegriffe) for talking about texts (here: "a comment")

4) A **one-paragraph summary** of an argumentative text (here: the first half of a comment), based on concepts of text interpretation for argumentation (CF. II, 10–11 AND III, 10–11), will make use of the following concepts: the given facts, the arguments for the writer's thesis, the counter-arguments for the antithesis, and conclusions from the opposed arguments. The summary is given of the following text:

Riots and the dangerous classes
After a great riot (Krawall, Aufruhr), there is much to be cleared away: the rubble (Trümmer), the burned-out cars, the broken glass. *But* then, for weeks afterwards, there is work to do clearing away the thick layer (Schicht) of nonsense which sifts down (herunterrieseln) like ash from the stratosphere upon us all. It is familiar nonsense. We hear that the fearful events at Brixton [1981, 1985] and Broadwater Farm [London, 1985] *were "mere criminality,"* that they *were instigated* (anzetteln) *by professional agitators* (the old "stormy petrel" [Sturmvogel] theory which has attended every disturbance for centuries). We hear that it was all the fault of the police or, *conversely* (umgekehrt), the natural con-

Preparing the summary
a) Underline references to the *given fact* (here: "a great riot", "the fearful events at Brixton and Broadwater Farm", etc.)

b) Find and underline references to the view the writer opposes (here: the *thesis* that rioting is not English; cf. "nonsense")

c) Mark the passages where the evidence (Beweise) for the opposed thesis is given (here: "were 'mere criminality'", "instigated by professional agitators", etc.)

sequence of harbouring (beheimaten) an alien (fremd), "ungovernable" race in British cities. We hear the tragic, understandable cry of a policeman: *"This isn't England!"*

But it is. Rioting is at least as English as thatched cottages (riedgedecktes Landhaus) and honey still for tea. *It is right to be appalled* (entrüstet) when young men – black and white together – burn, loot (plündern) and rape (vergewaltigen) and fight the police with petrol bombs, knives and guns. *But* it is badly wrong to conclude that we are entering unknown territory, that a violent break has been made with some "law-abiding" (Gesetze achtend), gentle (sanft) past of plebeian Britain to which intellectuals like Orwell, Leavis, even T. S. Eliot, used to appeal.

d) Find and underline references to the view the writer himself proposes (vorschlagen) (here: the *antithesis* that rioting *is* English)
e) Mark those passages where the writer concedes (zugestehen, einräumen) that the opposed view is or may be right (here: "It is right to be appalled...")
f) Look for *contrastive signals* (here: "But") which show the dialectical order of arguments for and against a view (here: "it is badly wrong to...")

Before the organisation of a proper police, there were countless popular explosions, from the Gordon riots of 1780 which left over 200 dead in London to upheavals (Aufstände) like the Reform riots in Bristol in 1831. People spoke then about "the dangerous classes," about "human vermin" (Ungeziefer) and "moral sewage" (Abwässer). The London police were first issued with firearms in 1883, when 821 officers received training in their use. There was Luddism (Bewegung der Maschinenzerstörung durch Arbeitslose, benannt nach Ned Ludd), the "Captain Swing" movement in the countryside, the Rebecca riots in rural (ländlich) Wales.

g) Mark the passages where the *evidence* for the writer's proposed view is given (here: from the time "Before the organization of a proper police"; use of a report in an argumentative text; cf. I, "Rule 3")

But in *"modern times," within living memory,* the tradition has persisted. This country was torn by violence in 1919, for example. First came the race riots against black seamen, which flared (aufflackern) around all the major sea-ports. Then came the outbreak

h) Mark further passages where the evidence for the writer's view is given (here: from "'modern times', within living memory")

in Luton, when crowds burned the town hall with petrol; there were over 100 casualties (Tote u. Verletzte) and troops had to be brought in. The next month, the police went on strike in Liverpool, and there followed days and nights of fighting and looting, put down by troops who had to charge with the bayonet while tanks moved into the Scotland Road area. All through that summer, crowds of young people challenged and fought the police in London – in Brixton, Tottenham and Wood Green, among other places.

Hoses against the mobs

There were unemployed riots *in 1921,* and much bigger outbreaks *in 1931.* In Manchester, the Army was called out in support of the civil power, and the police used high-pressure hoses (Feuerwehrschläuche) against the mobs. In Glasgow, the police attacked a demonstration of 50,000 people on Glasgow Green, precipitating (auslösen) a huge riot in which there was widespread looting and the storming of defended tenement blocks (Mietskasernen).

i) Further evidence for the writer's view

Behind these full-scale riots, potential violence simmered (schmoren) permanently in the poorest quarters of the cities. This was thought deplorable (bedauernswert), but not a cause for panic. Sir Robert Mark, in his memoirs, remembers violent street battles in Manchester as he – then a plain copper on the beat (einfacher Schutzmann auf seiner Runde) – went in for an arrest. But to him there was something "cheerful" about it. In such tumults, accompanied by drunkenness and looting at times (gelegentlich), "a good time was had by all."

j) Find and underline the passages where the writer begins to generalise and to draw *conclusions* from his evidence (here: "Behind *these ... riots,* potential violence simmered *permanently*", "not a cause for panic")

Rioting, in short, is one of the instruments of British political behaviour. It is a terrifying instrument, not often used, *but* it is the *traditional resort of those who feel excluded and oppressed by the social and political structure under which* – rather than in which – *they live.*
[...]
(NEAL ASCHERSON, IN: *THE OBSERVER,* 13 OCT., 1985)

k) Find and underline the passage where the writer returns to his thesis and draws the main conclusions from his evidence (here: "Rioting, *in short, is...*")

The **one-paragraph summary** of this article could read like this:

In the quoted part of his article, "Riots and the dangerous classes" (*The Observer,* 13 Oct. 1985), Neal Ascherson deals with the question whether *the 1985 riots at Brixton and Broadwater Farm in London* were really something quite un-English. To him it is "nonsense" to explain the riots *in terms of* criminality, agitation, a failure of the police, or of an ungovernable alien race (i.e. Blacks) in British cities. *In Ascherson's view,* rioting is in fact a traditional instrument of those in Britain "who feel excluded and oppressed" by the established political power structure. *Ascherson supports* his view with a wealth of historical *evidence,* from the Gordon riots of 1780 to the unemployed riots of 1921 and 1931.

a) Identification of the author and his publication (author's name, kind of text, title; if necessary: place, publisher, and year or date of publication)
b) Use of a summary expression (here: "the question whether") to point to the opposed views
c) Naming the given fact (here: "the 1985 riots") to which the opposed views (see b) refer
d) If necessary, reduction of the evidence to the topical keywords (here: "criminality", "agitation", etc.)
e) Use of opening signals to contrast the opposed view with the writer's (proposed) view (here: "In Ascherson's view")
f) Use of opening signals to refer to the writer's evidence
g) If necessary, reduction of the evidence to a summary expression (here: "a wealth of historical evidence") and only one or two examples

General steps for writing a summary

1) Read the text you want to sum up slowly with attention to detail.

2) Read the text again, underline **topical keywords** and give **headings** to the main subdivisions of the text. (Use your knowledge of text forms and text form language for recognizing important signals in the text.)

3) Write a **topic outline** (CF. II, 6) and give the lines, paragraphs, or pages for each topic.

4) If you are not familiar with the technical terms for talking about the kind of text before you (see [5] below), you can write a coherent summary that is based only on your **topic outline.** For a short summary of usually one paragraph, use opening and closing signals to compose a clear paragraph (CF. I, "RULE 3").

For a longer summary (of, for instance, a long article, a short story, novel, or play), compose your summary in a number of distinct (klar erkennbar) paragraphs. Each paragraph then sums up long passages of the original text.

5) If you are familiar with the technical terms and text form language for talking about the kind of text before you, you can also write your summary with the help of these **concepts of text interpretation.** Concepts such as setting, action, plot for narrative text forms, or problem, given fact, thesis or evidence and conclusion for argumentative text forms (CF. II, 10–11), can be used to order the ideas and topics of the original text in a clear and brief (knapp) summary. For texts of book length, you can use one or several paragraphs, depending on (je nach) the purpose of your summary (CF. "SOME AREAS OF USE"). The following sentences from a summary show the use of **technical terms for narrative texts:**

Hemingway's short story "Old Man at the Bridge" is *set in* Spain *at the time of* the Civil War from 1936–39. The *action is generated by* a soldier at a bridge... (CF. II, 2)

The use of **technical terms for argumentative texts** can be seen in these sentences from a summary:

Neal Ascherson deals with the question whether *[problem]* the 1985 riots at Brixton and Broadwater Farm in London *[given fact]* were really something quite un-English *[the opposed view/thesis]*. To him it is "nonsense" *[the proposed view/antithesis]* to explain the riots in terms of criminality, agitation... *[summary of the opposed evidence]* (CF. II, 10)

6) Use the tenses of the **present tense group** (CF. II, 2, "GENERAL STEPS", [5]), even when you sum up narrative texts.

Hemingway's "Old Man at the Bridge" *introduces* the reader to a dangerous situation at a bridge. Many people *are fleeing* across it, except an old man...

7) Sum up direct speech passages (dialogue) by **summary expressions** and **monologue.** (Do not use long passages of indirect speech).

...On returning, he [the narrator] enters into *a conversation* with the old man. He tries to *persuade* him to move on with the other refugees. But the old man's *thoughts are with* the few animals he had to leave behind...

8) Use **opening and closing signals** to compose clear **paragraphs** (CF. I, "RULE 3"). Combine your opening signal with an identification of the author, the kind of text, and title; if necessary, also give the place, publisher, and date of publication.

In the quoted part of *his article,* "Riots and the dangerous classes" (*The Observer,* 13 Oct. 1985), Neal Ascherson deals with...

(CF. "TEXT FORM DICTIONARY", III, 7.)

Some areas of use

Summaries are used:
a) to illustrate a point in a **long argumentative text,** for instance, in a **comment;** it can here serve as **evidence** for an argument.
This is the **comment** made as part of a longer article:

> [...] Years ago, people used to talk and write darkly about the "Americanisation" of Europe. If they no longer do, is it because we are already Americanised? Yes and no.

A **linking introduction** (verknüpfende Einleitung, Überleitung) is used to announce the summary:

> Part of my holiday reading has been an early novel by Malcolm Bradbury, "Stepping Westward." Written about a quarter of a century ago, this, too, recalled (wieder in Erinnerung rufen) how much has changed – in Britain.

Then the **summary** is given:

> A fattish, not very angry young writer goes to the States on a Fulbright (Fulbright-Stipendium). He leaves Nottingham by steam train, and crosses the Atlantic by liner complete with stewards handing round beef tea (Brühe). He reaches an utterly strange continent: here are universities with cement towers and wooden hutments (Baracken), students who go to lectures in their own towers, couples in ranch-style houses with patios (Terrassen), extractor fans (Ventilatoren) which start when the bathroom door opens, dental floss (Zahnseide), paper cups, supermarkets, hot showers in private bathrooms. Everyone is obsessed with sex, and everyone wants to be masterless.

After the summary, the **comment** is continued:

> So strange? It was then. Now it sounds like prosperous life in outer Richmond or outer Stirling – or Fontenay-les-Roses, or the new suburbs of Bonn. A gap has closed. The United States no longer seems marvellously unfamiliar. It impresses a European by its wealth and space, its Rocky Mountains and military power. *But not* its newness; we have the gadgets too, sometimes better ones, and gawky (unbeholfen) adaptations of the lifestyle.
>
> (Neal Ascherson, "The strange death of the peasantry", *The Observer,* 22 June 1986, p. 7)

b) to illustrate a concept in a long expository text, for instance, in a **text interpretation;**
c) as a brief introduction to a longer **research paper** (wissenschaftliche Abhandlung, Referat). This kind of summary is called an **abstract.** It sums up the paper before the paper itself begins.

8. Summarizing minutes

Definition: Summarizing minutes (zusammenfassendes [Ergebnis-]Protokoll) are a special kind of summary (cf. II, 7). We use summarizing minutes to sum up the results of spoken texts, for instance, the content of a talk or discussion.
Unlike summaries generally, summarizing minutes have a more or less fixed (festgelegt) composition. In their most detailed form, introductory headings are listed. By convention they identify:

- the type of meeting,
- the place and the date of the meeting,
- the participants (Teilnehmer), and
- the topics that were discussed, i.e. the agenda.

In the more informal situation of the classroom, summarizing minutes usually only identify the following aspects by introductory headings:

- the type of discussion (for instance: “Text interpretation of Hemingway, ‘At Two o’clock in the Morning’ – 4”),
- a numbered outline of the topics that were discussed.

These introductory headings are then followed by a summary of the main results for each of the listed topics. Summarizing minutes have an analytical order and are written in the tenses of the present tense group (cf. II, 2).

Forms

The following two texts illustrate the differences in composition for minutes 1) in a **formal situation** and 2) in a more **informal situation:**
1) Compositional plan for the **formal minutes** of a meeting, seminar, or conference:

Public Thoroughfares Committee Minutes of meeting held	a) type of meeting
at ...	b) place
on ...	c) date
Present: ..., Chairman ..., Deputy Chairman	d) alphabetical list of names of participants
Apologies [for absence] were received from Mrs. ...	e) names of expected participants who are absent
Agenda: 1. Minutes of meeting held on ... 2. Report by Mr. ... 3. Discussion of the report ... 7. Date of next meeting	f) topics in a numbered list

The name of the secretary (Protokollant) who keeps the minutes may be added in a separate heading after the agenda (“Secretary: ...”).

2) Compositional plan for **classroom minutes** of a text interpretation:

Ernest Hemingway, "At Two o'clock in the Morning"
(A summary of the text interpretation – 2)

a) The type of discussion, with a number for the first, second, third, etc. meeting/lesson (here: "– 2")

Topics: 1. Boyle's way of acting
2. Boyle's use of his gun
3. His powers as a policeman

b) A numbered outline of the topics discussed (i.e. the agenda)

1. Boyle's way of acting

In our last lesson (In our lesson of .. June, 19..), we discussed the way Boyle acts in Hemingway's short short story "At Two o'clock in the Morning". Our view was that Boyle's way of acting in the outlined situation has to be strongly condemned. At least the following two reasons can support this view.

2. Boyle's use of his gun

The first reason is connected with the particular situation in which Boyle uses his gun. Policemen carry guns chiefly because they must be able to defend themselves if they are threatened by armed criminals. Moreover, they may use their guns if a dangerous criminal tries to evade arrest by running away. In Boyle's situation, none of these circumstances apply.

3. His powers as a policeman

Our second reason is linked with a policeman's powers in society generally. It is the task of the police force in democratically organized societies to protect and defend law and order. However, a policeman's powers are strongly limited in this respect. Above all, a policeman is not allowed to punish a criminal. This is a power reserved to courts of law. In the situation outlined by Hemingway's story, Boyle obviously abuses his powers by passing the death sentence on the Hungarians.

For these reasons we can say that Boyle ought to be charged with murder. He has himself become a criminal.

General steps for writing summarizing minutes

1) Listen attentively to what is being said and take notes of the **main topics** and of **topical keywords** and expressions. Use shortened sentences (for instance, of only verbal groups for a known topic) and your own abbreviations (Abkürzungen) for fast speech. The **notes** taken for the minutes above could read like this:

> Boyle's way of acting? – Uses his gun – policemen in US carry guns – must be able to defend themselves – may use their guns against dangerous "criminals". Sum: does not apply in B.'s situation...

2) If a text is discussed (as in an interpretive discourse [Interpretationsgespräch]), mark those passages, lines or expressions which are quoted (zitieren) in connection with important conclusions (Schlußfolgerungen). Take a note also of the page, line and keyword(s).

> See ll. ... ff.: "Boyle *shot* one *off*..." = without warning...

3) Order your notes into an **outline** of main topics and subtopics (CF. II, 6). Use technical terms, for instance, for talking about argumentative text forms to group your notes (CF. II, 10–11 AND III, 10–11).

> *Two reasons*... The *first* reason... The *second* reason... *For these reasons*...

4) On the basis of your notes and outline (see 1–3 above), write a coherent (zusammenhängend) summarizing minute. To refer to your lesson, use the past tense and references to the participants only in your opening sentence, e.g. "In our last lesson, we discussed...". Then continue with the tenses of the **present tense group** (CF. II, 2, "GENERAL STEPS", [5]) and choose topical keywords as the subjects of your sentences. In other words, avoid giving a report (CF. II, 3) in the past tense group with personal subjects, e.g. "*Later we* said that...".

> ...Our view *was* that Boyle's way of acting in the outlined situation *has* to be strongly condemned. At least the following two reasons *can* support this view...

(CF. "TEXT FORM DICTIONARY", III, 8.)

Some areas of use

Summarizing minutes are used:
a) generally to keep a **written and approved** (angenommen) **record** (Aufzeichnung) of speech events (Sprechereignisse). They enable members and newcomers to bring themselves up to date (sich wieder ins Bild setzen) on what was said in the past.
b) in the classroom and seminar 1) to keep a written record of an interpretive discourse (Interpretationsgespräch) for later revision, 2) to learn and practise basic writing techniques, such as needed for individual written tasks in English text interpretation. Summarizing minutes can be based on the results and language of the collective effort (gemeinsame Bemühung) in text interpretation.

9. Text interpretations

Definition: In a text interpretation (Textdeutung, -interpretation) we give a longer explanation of the ideas and suggestions (Andeutungen) which are contained in a text and which are not immediately clear to a reader.

Usually, we write a text interpretation to explain a text for readers who are not among the competent readers or listeners to whom the author first spoke. An article from a British newspaper of today needs an interpretation for most German readers. A British newspaper article of 1968 will need an interpretation even for most British readers.

Generally, we can follow two different approaches (Verfahren, Vorgehensweisen) in text interpretations. In **inductive text interpretation** ([von Einzelnem] herleitende Textinterpretation), we closely follow the meanings and suggestions of the words, sentences, and composition of a text. To put it differently, we link (verknüpfen) the words of a text with our knowledge of language and the world.

In **deductive text interpretation** ([von Allgemeinem] ableitende Textinterpretation), we start from some general concept.

We then explain how this concept can be linked with certain particular aspects and passages of the text. In other words, we use the concept that we know as a guideline for reading and explaining a text.

In a longer text interpretation, we usually mix our explanations with passages in which we give a summary (CF. II, 7), a definition (CF. II, 4), an explication (CF. II, 5), a topic outline (CF. II, 6), or a comment (CF. II, 10). Text interpretations have an analytical order and are written in the tenses of the present tense group (CF. II, 2). They are connected with comprehension.

Forms

The following two text interpretations can illustrate how we write an inductive and a deductive text interpretation:

1) For an inductive text interpretation we can start from the following short poem on autumn:

T. E. Hulme, Autumn

A touch of cold in the Autumn night –
I walked abroad,
And saw the ruddy moon lean over a hedge
Like a red-faced farmer.
I did not stop to speak, but nodded,
And round about were the wistful stars
With white faces like town children.

A paragraph of the **inductive text interpretation** may read like this:

▭ As the main verbs indicate – (see "walked abroad", "saw" and "did not stop"), the speaker presents himself in this poem in the role of somebody taking a walk one autumn night (l. 1: "in the Autumn night"). ⊟ The adverb "abroad" shows the direction that the speaker takes. He walks away from the limiting confines of a house, perhaps, into an area of gardens and fields with "hedge[s]" (l. 3) ⊡ until he has an unobstructed view of the night sky: "And *round about* were the wistful stars" (l. 6)...

▭ Beginning
a) Words or expressions that form topical (thematisch) connections in the interpreted text (here: the verbs "walked abroad", etc.)
b) Use of a generalizing (verallgemeinernd) expression for the topical connection (here: "the speaker", "somebody taking a walk")

⊟ Middle
c) The general insight (Einsicht) and the world of objects and ideas that we know (here: "The adverb 'abroad' shows the direction", "away from...", etc.)
d) Use of explicatory (erklärend) signals from time to time (here: "indicate", "see", "shows")

⊡ End
e) Observations from the end of a topical line in the text (here: from the last two lines of the poem)

2) For a deductive text interpretation we can look at the following text on a play (Arthur Miller, Death of a Salesman).
The general concept that the writer starts from is presented in this question:

What is the pattern of the father-son relationships in the play?

This is the **deductive text interpretation** that follows:

▭ The frequent mirroring of *father-son relationships* reinforces the fact that "Death of a Salesman" is primarily a drama about *the conflict between Willy and Biff*.
⊟ In the dim past there was Willy's *father* and his *two sons;* the father was an itinerant flute-maker, a creative man who traveled to the western frontiers and to Alaska. The older brother Ben followed in his footsteps and became rich, but Willy remembers him only as "a man with a big beard, and I was in Mamma's lap". (p. 157) *When* Linda soothes Willy to sleep with a lullaby *we see that* Willy has never been able to wean himself from the need of a mother-figure – he drinks milk to soothe his nerves. And he suppresses the artisan in him, the skill of making things with his hands that he inherited from his father. *When* Biff resolves to

▭ Beginning
a) A general concept that can guide the observations in the interpreted text (here: "father-son relationships")
b) Illustration of the guiding concept from the interpreted text (here: "the conflict between Willy and Biff")

⊟ Middle
c) The introductory concept and passages in the text that can illustrate it further (here: "Willy's *father* and his two *sons*", etc.)
d) Brief summary or quotation of relevant passages from the text (here: "When Linda soothes Willy to sleep...", etc.)
e) Explanation and evaluation (Bewertung) of the quoted passages (here: "we see that Willy has...")
f) Use of explicatory signals from time to time to show the analytical order of the text interpretation (here: "we see that")
g) Passages from the interpreted text which enable (ermöglichen) others to follow and accept the conclusions. In other words, use of an objective point of view (here: "When Biff resolves to break with his parents and go to Texas, he...")

break with his parents and go to Texas, he is reverting back to the healthy drives of his grandfather; but Happy remains in the grip of his Oedipal ties – he denies his father *in the restaurant scene,* but resolves to fulfill his father's dream *in the Requiem scene*. And his attachment to his mother is so strong that he cannot genuinely love another woman.

☐ Two other father-son relationships figure in the play: Old Man Wagner and his son Howard, and Charley and his son Bernard.

(J. V. HAGOPIAN AND M. DOLCH, *INSIGHT I.* FRANKFURT, 1962, P. 183)

☐ End
h) Observations from the end of the topical line that has been followed through the text (here: "resolves to fulfill his father's dream in the Requiem scene")

General steps for writing a text interpretation

A. An **inductive text intrepretation:**

1) Look for individual words and sentences in a text by which the writer creates **topical connections** in parts of the text or in the whole text. You may want to mark these topical expressions by underlining in different parts of the text. In short texts, link them by lines, so that you can easily work with them.

As the *main verbs indicate* (see "walked abroad", "saw", and "did not stop"), …

2) Find generalizing words, terms or expressions to explain each topical connection or line in the text. In this way, the underlined topical expressions become **illustrations** of the new **generalizing term.**

As the main verbs indicate (*see* "walked abroad", "saw", and "did not stop"), the speaker *presents himself* in this poem in *the role of somebody taking a walk…*

3) Link your general insight with what else it can tell you about **the world of objects or ideas** that you know. Use the text as a guide. Steps 1 and 2 could give this particular insight:

…The adverb "abroad" *shows the direction* that the speaker takes [i. e. on his "walk"].

Step 3 could lead to these further particular explanations:

He walks *away from the limiting confines of a house,* perhaps, *into an area of gardens and fields* with "hedge[s]" (l. 3) until he has an *unobstructed view of the night sky:* "And *round about* were the wistful stars" (l. 6)…

4) Use **explicatory** ([ek'splıkətərı], erklärend) **signals** from time to time to link your particular insights with a general insight, or the other way round.

As the main verbs *indicate… (see…)*
The adverb "abroad" *shows* the direction that…

5) Now use your first insights as a guideline when looking for further topical connections in the text. Repeat the **topical keyword** as an opening **long-distance signal** (CF. ALSO II, 5) to help the reader remember the elements and topics you have already mentioned some time before.

On his walk, the speaker has an unusual experience. It is connected with *where he saw the moon.* As is characteristic of its positions and appearance in autumn, the speaker saw the moon low on the horizon, so that it appeared to "lean over a hedge" (l. 3)…

B. A **deductive text interpretation:**
1) Choose and start from a **general concept** to guide your observations (Beobachtungen) in a text. You can choose these concepts from two different areas:
a) from your knowledge of the world of objects and thought; these are **thematic concepts:**

What is the pattern of the *father-son relationships* in Arthur Miller's "Death of a Salesman"?

b) from your knowledge about how texts are composed of words, paragraphs, certain orders, etc.; these are **concepts of text forms and language** or **literary concepts.**

Where in Miller's play does the final *crisis* occur?
The final *crisis* occurs when Willy and Biff meet at home that evening. Biff tells his mother, "with absolute assurance, determination: 'We're gonna have an abrupt conversation, him and me.'" (p. 211) Biff does not intend to…

2) Look for only those **passages in the text** that refer to the chosen concept. Briefly sum up these passages in a clause, sentence or paragraph, so that the general concept is **illustrated** (CF. II, 7).

When Linda soothes Willy to sleep with a lullaby, we see that Willy has never been able to wean himself from the need of a mother-figure…
When Biff resolves to break with his parents and go to Texas, he is reverting back to the healthy drives of his grandfather; but Happy remains in the grip of his Oedipal ties – *he denies his father in the restaurant scene,* but…

3) **Explain and evaluate** (bewerten, beurteilen) what the marked and summed up passages tell you about the chosen general concept.

When Biff resolves to break with his parents and go to Texas, *he is reverting back to the healthy drives of his grandfather;…*

4) Use **explicatory signals** from time to time to link your illustrative quotations and summaries of passages (see 2 above) with your general topical concept.

> When Linda soothes Willy to sleep with a lullaby, *we see that* Willy has never been able to wean himself from the need of a mother-figure...

5) Write your text interpretations from a predominantly (vorwiegend) **objective point of view,** so that others can follow and perhaps accept your explanations and conclusions. Your **subjective views** can be added in those passages of your text interpretations where you comment on your results (CF. II, 10).

> On the basis of your results, would you say that Miller's play is an anti-capitalistic play?
> Arthur Miller himself has denied it. "A play", he says, "cannot be equated with (gleichsetzen mit) a political philosophy..." I *think it must be admitted that* in its larger dimensions, this play is not primarily concerned with politics or economics. *Nevertheless,* to the extent that (in dem Maße, wie) it is concerned with these matters, the play is *clearly* an indictment (Anklage) of the profit motive, and competitive salesmanship, and planned obsolescence (geplantes Veralten)... (HAGOPIAN/DOLCH, P. 182; SHORTENED)

(CF. "TEXT FORM DICTIONARY", III, 9.)

Some areas of use

Text interpretations are used:
a) to help others to understand a text, especially a long text that they may not fully understand – because they lack the **thematic background knowledge** of the author's intended readers/listeners; or because they cannot easily understand the **composition and language** of the text (for instance, of a poem or long comment); or because they are not familiar with (nicht vertraut sein mit) the **special field of knowledge** that the text was written about (for instance, statutes [Gesetze]).
b) in **foreign language learning,** to improve one's command of the language (Sprachbeherrschung) and, at the same time, to acquire (erwerben) knowledge about the world in which we live, especially about people and their environments in the countries where the foreign language is spoken.

Argumentative text forms

In argumentative ([ˌɑːgjʊ'mentətɪv], erörternd) text forms we make j u d g m e n t s (Urteile fällen). We say how, in our view (unserer Ansicht nach), something (i. e. a given fact or idea) should be evaluated (bewerten). We take one view, and give reasons for this view, and so usually speak against a different view. In short, we discuss the two sides of an i s s u e (Problem).

When we try to persuade (überreden) others to our view, with the help of personal arguments for or against something, we make a **comment.** Comments are a subjective form of argumentation.
Argumentation with arguments that can be verified (bewahrheiten, überprüfen) by others as objective evidence (Beweis[e]) is called **formal argumentation** (formale, wissenschaftliche Argumentation).
Common (verbreitet) argumentative text forms are leading articles (Leitartikel), reviews (Besprechungen, Rezensionen) of books, films or plays, personal statements (persönliche Stellungnahmen), letters to the editor, research papers (Referate, wissenschaftliche Abhandlungen), satirical cartoons on politicians, and discussions on TV, debates in parliament, or parts of interviews where someone is asked his or her opinion (Meinung) on a matter.
Argumentative passages are often also used as part of a text interpretation (CF. II, 9).

10. Comments

Definition: In a comment (Stellungnahme, Kommentar), we state (nennen, vortragen) our opinions (Meinungen) and personal views on something. Usually, we make a judgment by "yes" or "no" to show how we answer a difficult question or a problem. We have to make a choice.
In a personal comment, we usually state first whether we are for or against something. Then we give reasons, or arguments, for our view, usually in opposition to a different view. We usually finish with a conclusion (Schlußfolgerung) based on the evidence (Beweisführung) that we have given.
When we develop a comment by moving from reasons for a view to reasons against it, then to other reasons for and against it and so on, we follow a d i a l e c t i c a l o r d e r (in Gegensätzen entwickelte Folge). This dialectical order is based on contrasts and comparisons.

Forms

The following texts illustrate how we can express ourselves in shorter or longer comments. We refer to a literary text and use it to make judgments on the way certain characters behave towards each other (SEE HEMINGWAY, "AT TWO O'CLOCK IN THE MORNING", II, 2).

1) Making a **one-sentence comment.** It may be used as part of a longer text interpretation (CF. II, 9) that starts from this question:

What view do you take of Boyle shooting the two Hungarians?

The short comment may read like this:

I think Boyle is a murderer *because* he acts against the law.

a) Use of a viewpoint expression (here: "I think") and statement of the view taken for a certain evaluation (here: "is")
b) Support of the stated view with a reason (here: a causal clause [Nebensatz des Grundes])

2) A **one-paragraph comment** might take this form:

⬒ In Hemingway's story "At Two o'clock in the Morning", Drevitts comments on Boyle's shooting of the two Hungarians, "That's all right maybe this time." ⊟ *In my view, however,* Boyle should be strongly condemned (verurteilen) for his way of acting. *Surely,* Boyle does not care about the law of the country. As a policeman in a democratic society he ought to protect (schützen) the law. *But* Boyle acts against the law not to kill. He abuses (mißbrauchen) his powers as a policeman when he does not arrest the two Hungarians. He ought to wait for the courts (Gerichte) to pass sentence (Gerichtsurteil fällen) on the two burglars. ⬓ He has no right to use his gun and take the law into his own hands. *So, to my mind,* Boyle is a murderer.

⬒ Beginning
a) The given fact that can be viewed in different ways (here: "Boyle's shooting of the two Hungarians")
b) Quotation or summary of the view that is opposed (widersprechen). This is the thesis (Ausgangsbehauptung).

⊟ Middle
c) The view that is taken and defended against the thesis. This is the antithesis (Gegenbehauptung).
d) Use of contrastive (entgegensetzend) signals to show the dialectical order of the comment (here: "however", "but")
e) Use of adverbs that show the writer's attitude (attitudinal adverbs [Adverbien der Einstellung]) and are meant to persuade the listener (here: "surely")
f) Reasons for the writer's view from the world of everyday experience (Erfahrungswelt), from general knowledge, from the text, or from other texts; combined with an appeal to values (Wertvorstellungen)

⬓ End
g) A general conclusion from the arguments and final summary of the writer's view (here: "is a murderer")

3) Using a **comment as an argumentative frame** to a text interpretation. The text interpretation is used as evidence (Beweisführung) for the writer's view (here: of how Drevitts behaves in Hemingway's story).
The opening part of the **comment** could state the writer's view like this:

⬒ *I think that* Drevitts markedly (['mɑ:kɪdlɪ], deutlich) differs from Boyle. Drevitts's choice of words in his comment in l. … *clearly* shows that he fears they will be held responsible (zur Verantwortung ziehen) and will perhaps even be charged with the killings.

⬒ Beginning
a) Use of a viewpoint expression (here: "I think") and statement of the writer's view for or against another view (here: "differs")
b) Support of the writer's view with an argument from the text (here: "His choice of words … in l. …")
c) Support of the writer's view with attitudinal adverbs (here: "clearly")

The **text interpretation** used as evidence in the argumentative frame might make the following point:

⊟ When Drevitts says to Boyle, "you oughtn't to have done it" (l. …), his choice of the auxiliary "oughtn't to"

⊟ Middle
d) Connection of the stated view with passages in the text that can explain and illustrate it further

points to a moral obligation (Verpflichtung). *Similarly,* when he says, "There's *liable to* be a hell of a lot of trouble" (*see* l. . . .), "be liable" *indicates that* he knows that these killings cannot be easily justified (rechtfertigen) by them before their superiors (Vorgesetzte) or before a lawcourt (Gericht).

e) Brief summary or quotation of relevant passages from the text
f) Explanation and evaluation of the quoted passages (here: "points to a moral obligation")
g) Use of explicatory (erklärend) signals from time to time to show the analytical order of the text interpretation (here: "similarly", "indicates that", CF. II, 9)

The closing part of the **comment** may read like this:

❑ *I think* in the illustrated reactions Drevitts can be seen to differ very strongly from his companion. Drevitts knows the law of the land and feels obliged (verpflichtet) to respect it.

❑ End
h) Return to the argumentative frame and use of a viewpoint expression to draw a general conclusion from the evidence (here: a text interpretation). Final statement of the writer's view in a new, summary way (here: "He knows the law ... and feels obliged to respect it")

General steps for writing a comment

Your paragraph or text	Beginning	Steps 1–4
	Middle	Steps 5–8
	End	Step 9

1) Think of the **given fact or idea** with which opposing (einander widersprechend) views are or can be connected. Use the given fact/idea as the topic or **problem** to start from.

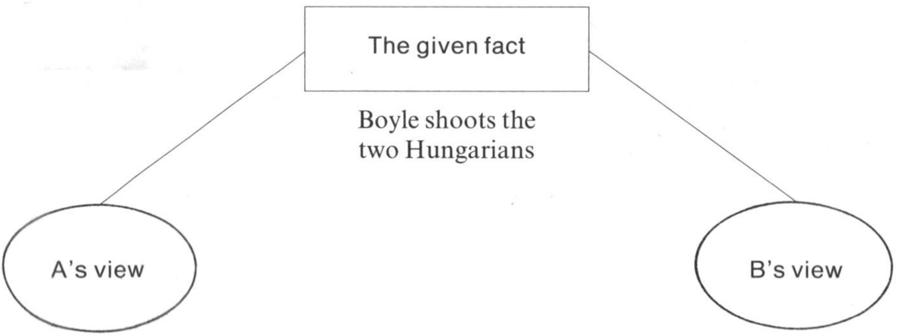

Boyle shoots the two Hungarians

Drevitts comments, "That's all right maybe this time." . . . . **BUT** . . . . in my view Boyle should be strongly condemned for . . .

2) Quote or sum up the **view** that you want **to oppose** (ablehnen). Inform your reader/listener about the **thesis** that you cannot accept.

Drevitts says/comments, "That's all right maybe this time."

3) Then state **your own view.** Use it as the **antithesis** that you support and defend. Support your view with at least two pieces of evidence (CF. ALSO II, 11, "GENERAL STEPS", 8 ON USING A BLOCK-BUILDING OUTLINE).
You may introduce the statement of your own view a) with a contrastive signal such as "however", "but", "yet" (doch); b) with a viewpoint expression such as "I think", "I don't think", "In my view", etc.

In my view, however, Boyle should be strongly condemned for his way of acting.

4) You may give **emphasis** (Nachdruck) to your point of view **by attitudinal adverbs** such as "surely", "clearly", "obviously" (offensichtlich), "no doubt" (zweifellos).

Surely, Boyle does not care about the law of the land.

*

5) Give **reasons** for your view: from the world of everyday experience, from general knowledge, from the text, or from other texts you have read. In a comment, you may also appeal to (appellieren an) the needs (Bedürfnisse) and values (Wertvorstellungen) of people.

As a policeman *in a democratic society* [general knowledge] he *ought to protect the law* [appeal to values].
He abuses *his powers as a policeman* when he does not *arrest* the two Hungarians [general knowledge].

6) In your argumentation, you may also want to use the following kinds of clauses. They are typical of argumentative text forms:

a) **causal clauses** with "since" (da [ja]), "as" (da), or "because" to introduce reasons:

Since Drevitts uses words like "oughtn't to" and "liable to", we can say that he feels a moral obligation to condemn Boyle's way of acting.

b) **concessive clauses** (einräumende Nebensätze) to include objections (Einwände) to your view; they are introduced by "although" (obwohl, obgleich), "though" (obwohl):

Though Drevitts accepts Boyle's way of acting in the end, he does feel (fühlt er sich doch) very uncomfortable (see his sentence, "That's all right maybe this time").

c) **conditional clauses** with "if", "unless" (wenn nicht), "in case" (für den Fall, daß). Conditional clauses can be used:

– to say what you think is *possible in the present* (Gegenwart) or in the future:
If Drevitts *did* not give in, Boyle *would* perhaps *kill* him, too.

conditional clause	main clause
past tense (I was – I had – I said – I called)	**conditional I** (I would/should say – I could say – I might say)

– to say what you think was *possible only in the past,* but is no longer possible now: *If* Boyle *had shot* Drevitts, nobody *would have known* who had killed him.

conditional clause	main clause
past perfect (I had been – I had had – I had said – I had called)	**conditional II** (I would have said – I could have said – I might have said)

Since we often think of possibilities in argumentative texts, it is very important to choose the correct sequence of tenses (Zeitenfolge; see the two diagrams above).

7) To introduce arguments for or against a view, you can also use **causal expressions** at the beginning of a sentence, such as:

The reason(s) for this is/are that… / This is why… (Deshalb) / There is every reason why… (Es gibt viele Gründe, warum) / There is no reason why… / Another reason why… is…

8) Use **contrastive signals** in the body of the text to continue and support the dialectical order of contrast and comparison in the text.

At the end of the story, Drevitts appears to have been deeply frightened by Boyle's threatening question of "Who the hell is going to make any trouble?" *By contrast* [= But], Boyle appears to be in a joking mood now when he says, "Wops, […] I can tell wops a mile off."

*

9) At the end of a paragraph or a longer comment, **draw a conclusion** (Schlußfolgerung) from your arguments. Try to state your view again in a new, summary way.
You may announce your conclusion by using signals for the end such as "so", "thus" (auf diese Weise), "therefore", "what I am saying is" (was ich sagen wollte, ist).

…He has no right to use his gun and take the law into his own hands. *So, to my mind,* Boyle *is a murderer.*

(cf. "Text form dictionary", III, 10)

Some areas of use

Comments are introduced, for instance, in the classroom:

a) when you state your view on a problem that is being discussed in the group. Usually, these are short, up to one-paragraph spoken comments. They may be based on a short

topical note that you have taken during the discussion while you were waiting to contribute (beitragen) to it.
The beginning of a spoken comment in a discussion might take this form:

> Returning to A's explanation of X as..., I would like to point to a passage on page... There it says (Dort heißt es) that "..." I fully/wholeheartedly (uneingeschränkt) *agree with A when he says that*... I completely/utterly (ganz und gar) *disagree with A, however, when he claims that*... Let me briefly illustrate the point I am making...

b) when you evaluate (bewerten) the results of a written text interpretation and state whether you agree or disagree with the suggestions in the text. While you must explain the text objectively in your explication, you are free to put forward your personal views and opinions in such added comments.

11. Formal argumentation

Definition: In formal argumentation (formale, wissenschaftliche Argumentation), we make judgments on a problem with arguments that can be verified objectively (objektiv überprüft/bewahrheitet werden) by others. To be able to evaluate (beurteilen) a matter objectively we use methods which follow the accepted principles (Grundsätze) of a scientific discipline. This is why we can also speak of "scientific argumentation".
Formal argumentation usually takes the form of a long research paper (wissenschaftliche Abhandlung, Referat) or a scholarly book (['skɒləlɪ], wissenschaftlich, gelehrt). However, elementary aspects of formal argumentation are also to be found, for instance, in those parts of a text interpretation (CF. II, 9), where we argue a certain view of a character's behaviour, or of how to understand a certain image (Bild), etc. When we support our view and interpretation with quotations from the text, or when we refer to other texts or books as sources (Quellen) of our interpretation (and list these references in footnotes and a bibliography [Literaturverzeichnis] of works we have consulted [zu Rate ziehen, nachschlagen]), then we give the kind of verifiable evidence that is also characteristic of a research paper.
Moreover, a long research paper or scholarly treatise in book form will begin with a table of contents that is based on a very detailed topic outline (CF. II, 6; SEE ALSO THE "TABLE OF CONTENTS" IN THIS BOOK). It is expected to end with an alphabetical list of key terms and, sometimes, of names (an index).

Forms

To illustrate the basic aspects of formal argumentation, which you may want to use, for instance, in a longer term paper (Referat), we can study the following paragraphs from a short formal argumentation on Arthur Miller's play "Death of a Salesman".
The **problem** for the argumentative frame is introduced by a question:

> "Is the play an anti-capitalistic play?"

The **formal argumentation,** with a text interpretation for evidence reads:

▭ Arthur Miller himself *has denied it* (leugnen, verneinen). "A play," he says, "cannot be equated (gleichsetzen) with a political philosophy... / ...To speak of a play as though it were the objective work of a propagandist is an almost biological kind of nonsense, provided (vorausgesetzt), of course, that it is a play, which is to say (das heißt) a work of art" (Cf. the author's introduction to the "Collected Plays", New York, 1957, pp. 36–38). He says further, "The most decent man in 'Death of a Salesman' is a capitalist (Charley) whose aims are not different from Willy Loman's. The great difference between them is that Charley is not a fanatic" ("Collected Plays," p. 37).

▭ Beginning
a) A summary of the view that the writer wants to oppose (here: summary of Miller's thesis; see "has denied it")
b) Use of quotations that could verify the summarized thesis
c) Identification of the writer's sources by name, title, place, and date of publication, with exact page references

⊟ And *it must be admitted that* in its larger dimensions, this play is not primarily (vorwiegend) concerned with (sich befassen mit) politics or economics. Nevertheless (Nichtsdestoweniger), *to the extent that* (in dem Maße wie) *it is concerned with these matters,* the play is clearly an indictment (Anklage) of the profit motive, and competitive salesmanship ([kəm'petɪtɪv], wettbewerbsorientierte Verkaufstechnik), and planned obsolescence (the deliberate [bewußt] manufacture [Herstellung] of goods which, for reasons of style or quality, will need to be replaced [ersetzen] after a short time) – the three principal (Haupt-) factors of capitalistic society that distinguish it from any other dehumanizing (entmenschlichend) industrial mass society. *When Willy is cruelly deprived of* (entziehen, wegnehmen) *his job after some forty years with the firm,* Howard explains, "It's a business, kid, and everybody's gotta pull his own weight... business is business" (p. 180). And Willy rightly protests against planned obsolescence:

⊟ Middle
d) Use of an impersonal (unpersönlich) point of view (here: use of viewpoint expressions with "it" plus passive voice)
e) Modification (Einschränkung) of the writer's assertions (Behauptungen) to show how valid (gültig) they are
f) Evidence for the writer's assertions from his own investigation (genaue Untersuchung) of the text (= explication and interpretation)
g) Quotation from the text and exact reference to the text edition and the pages from which the writer is quoting

"Once in my life I would like to own something outright (ganz) before it's broken! I'm always in a race with the junkyard! I just finished paying for the car and it's on its last legs. The refrigerator consumes belts (Treibriemen) like a goddam maniac (['meɪnɪæk], Irrer). They time those things. They time them so when you finally paid for them, they're used up" (p. 174).
Miller has said also that the exponents ([ɪk'spəʊnənts], Vertreter) of socialism cannot take heart from his work. "There is no such thing as a capitalistic assembly line (Fließband) or drygoods (Kurzwaren) counter. The disciplines required by machines are the same everywhere and will not be truly mitigated (mildern) by old-age pensions and social-security payments. So long as modern man conceives of himself (sich verstehen als) as valuable only because he fits into some niche (Nische) in the machine-tending pattern (im maschinenwartenden Muster), he will never know anything more than a pathetic doom (mitleiderregendes Schicksal)" ("On Social Plays", p. 10). There is truth in this, and "Death of a Salesman" is also an indictment of all modern industrial society; □ but, again, in specifically attacking the profit motive, competitive salesmanship, and planned obsolescence, this play does directly hit at the capitalistic form of modern society.

(John V. Hagopian and M. Dolch, *Insight I.* Frankfurt, 1962, p. 182; notes adapted)

□ End
h) A general conclusion drawn both from the opposed view and the writer's own arguments and investigation
i) Use of certain stylistic means (Stilmittel) for emphasis (Nachdruck; here: emphatic "do"; cf. III, 10, V, [6])

General steps for writing a piece of formal argumentation

Your paragraph or text	Beginning	Steps 1–2
	Middle	Steps 3–8
	End	Step 9

1) Think of the **given fact or idea** with which opposing (einander widersprechend) views are or can be connected. Use the given fact/idea as the topic or **problem** to start from.

The play is not anti-capitalistic. ...... **BUT** .... "to the extent that it is concerned with these matters", it *is* an indictment of capitalistic society

2) **Sum up and quote** the view that you want to oppose (the thesis). For verification (Überprüfung, Wahrheitsnachweis), identify your **sources** (Quellen) by author's name, title, place and date of publication, and add the exact page references for your quotations. In technical terms, these facts are known as **documentation** (Belege, Quellennachweise).
The end of the quotation reads:

> "...which is to say a work of art"

The documentation is added like this:

> (Cf. the author's [Arthur Miller's] introduction to the "Collected Plays," New York, 1957, pp. 36–38).

*

3) Then state your own view as an **antithesis.** Speak from an impersonal third-person point of view, for instance, by using **viewpoint expressions** with "it" plus the passive voice. Or simply use references to the matter under discussion as subjects of your sentences ("X is/is not...").
The viewpoint expression may introduce a sentence like this:

> And *it must be admitted* that in its larger dimensions, this play is not primarily concerned with politics or economics. *Nevertheless, to the extent that it is concerned with these matters,* the play *is clearly an indictment of...*

You may introduce the statement of your own view and arguments with a **contrastive** (entgegensetzend) **signal** such as "however", "but", "yet" (doch), "nevertheless".

> *Nevertheless,* [...] the play is clearly an indictment of the profit motive, and competitive salesmanship, and planned obsolescence...

4) Emphasis by **attitudinal adverbs** (such as "surely", "clearly", "obviously", "no doubt") is used more sparingly (sparsamer) in formal argumentation than in comments (CF. II, 10.).

Nevertheless, [...] the play is *clearly* an indictment of...

Similarly, emphatic "do" in affirmative sentences (in bejahten Sätzen) is only occasionally (gelegentlich) used, and then with reference not to the writer ("But *I* do think..."), but to an impersonal subject:

...*but* again, in specifically attacking the profit motive, competitive salesmanship, and planned obsolescence, *this play does* directly hit at the capitalistic form of modern society.

5) For a discussion of clauses in argumentative text forms **(causal, concessive,** and **conditional clauses),** cf. II, 10, "General steps", 6.

6) For a discussion of contrastive signals in the body of the text to continue and support the **dialectical order** of the text, cf. II, 10, "General steps", 8.

7) Give **evidence** for your assertions (Behauptungen). Collect pieces of evidence:
a) from your own **investigation,** for instance, a close reading of a text, or the results of interviews of various readers or spectators; these are your **primary sources** (Primärquellen).

When Willy is cruelly deprived of his job after some forty years with the firm, Howard explains, "It's a business, kid, and everybody's gotta pull his own weight ... business is business" (p. 180). And Willy rightly protests against planned obsolescence: "Once in my life I would like to own something outright before it's broken!..." (p. 174).

b) from what other investigators have found out in connection with the problem and published in scholarly papers or books; these are your **secondary sources** (Sekundärquellen).

Miller has said also that the exponents of socialism cannot take heart from his work. "There is no such thing as a capitalistic assembly line or drygoods counter..." ("On Social Plays", p. 10). There is truth in this...

Identify your references to the text (by its edition, page and/or lines) and to your secondary sources (by author's name, title, place and date of publication, and page reference).

8) Order your evidence with the help of an **outline** (CF. II, 6). You may want to group the reasons *for* a position in one block, the reasons *against* it in another, separate block. We speak, in such instances, of a **block-building outline**.
You can choose, for instance, a climactic order (CF. II, 2), so that the most important fact comes last in the outline:

Is "Death of a Salesman" an anti-capitalistic play?

For:	Against:
– Howard's explanation of why Willy is deprived of his job; see p. 180: "It's a business..."	...
– Willy's protest against planned obsolescence; see p. 174: "Once in my life..."	
– Miller's own indictment of all modern industrial society; see "On Social Plays", p. 10	

This is an example of a text based on a block-building outline of reasons for and against a question:

> *The debate over* pregnancy leave (Schwangerschaftsurlaub) has created a deep rift (Spaltung) among feminists.
> *One side argues that* pregnancy leave, even though it benefits individual women, poses a general danger to female workers because it singles them out (herausstellen) for special protection [= the first reason against]. Historically, they point out, such privileged treatment has eventually (am Ende) led to discrimination against women [= the second reason against]. Says Marsha Levick of the National Organization for Women's legal defense and education fund: "That [privileged treatment] almost always backfires [Nachteile bringen]."
> *But other feminists contend* pregnancy leave simply acknowledges women's child-bearing function and...
> ("TIME", JANUARY 26, 1987, P. 25)

*

9) Draw a **conclusion** from your arguments in the light of your opponent's view. Try to state your own view again in a new summary way.
You may announce your conclusion by **resultative signals** ([rɪ'zʌltətɪv], auf ein Ergebnis weisend), such as "so", "therefore", "in conclusion".
The summary, combined with emphasis on the writer's view, may read:

> ...*but, again,* in specifically attacking the profit motive, competitive salesmanship, and planned obsolescence, this play *does directly hit at* the capitalistic form of modern society.

(CF. "TEXT FORM DICTIONARY", III, 11.)

Some areas of use

Short pieces of formal argumentation are also used:
a) as parts of a longer **text interpretation** that has been prepared on the basis of scholarly papers or books on the same text (for instance, on a play, novel, short story, or poem) and is written as a **term paper;**
b) as part of a **prepared discussion** on a field of knowledge (e. g. historical events) that is connected with the English-speaking world.

Instructive text forms

In instructive (anweisend, anordnend, belehrend) texts we tell ourselves or other people what to do or how to behave. Instruction for certain kinds of future behaviour (zukünftiges Verhalten) is connected with planning.
In some situations, we can simply use a number of imperative sentences ("Get your tickets at this counter"); in other situations, however, we are expected to use the language of polite (höflich) style ("Please queue here for tickets").
All instructive text forms analyse (zerlegen) the planned behaviour into a sequence (Abfolge) of elements that can be listed. The characteristic connection between sentences in instructive texts is created by an analytical order (cf. II, 5) as well as a listing order.

12. Personal instructions and practical or statutory instruction

Definition: In everyday situations, we ourselves normally use various kinds of **personal instructions.** These are instructive text forms which are based on some kind of personal authority that we have – because of special knowledge (Wissen) or our experience (Erfahrung), or because of our status ([gesellschaftliche] Stellung) or role. Common longer text forms of this subjective kind of instruction are certain kinds of personal letter (e.g. for ordering something), business letters in commercial correspondence (Handelskorrespondenz), advertisements, various pieces of propaganda (e.g. political speeches), sermons (Predigten), or longer recommendations (Empfehlungen) as part of an argumentative essay.
Quite a number of other instructive text forms, however, are based on some impersonal (unpersönlich) authority outside and above ourselves. If demands (Forderungen) are based on the practical knowledge of how things work or behave, we speak of **practical instruction.** Directions (Anleitungen) on how to cook a particular meal or how to plant a pool in one's garden, are followed because of their practical value.
If demands are based on some kind of public authority, such as law-making institutions (parliaments), institutions that protect justice, i.e. lawcourts (Gerichte), and demand moral behaviour, such as lawcourts or the churches, we speak of **statutory instruction** (gesetzliche Instruktion). To this binding kind of instructive text forms belong rules (festgelegte Regeln; e.g. in football), regulations ([behördliche] Verordnungen), and statutes (Gesetze) generally.
We have to learn about the composition both of personal instructions and statutory instruction, even though we usually will not have to write statutory instruction ourselves. But we will often have to read and later report statutory instruction, for example, in parts of our text interpretations or longer comments. In such instances, it will help us to know what order to follow in our instructive text divisions and what expressions and sentence patterns to use.

Forms

The following texts illustrate how the language changes when we move from personal instructions to statutory instruction:

1) Short personal instructions as part of a comment on the convention (Sitte) of shaking hands upon introduction in Britain. The introductory **comment** may read like this:

> Some time ago all a woman *was expected to* do when someone was introduced to her was to smile, incline (neigen) her head and murmur "How do you do?" [...] *Although* it is still perfectly correct, this little nod today looks condescending (herablassend) and unfriendly, *unless* the woman is introduced to a group of people and cannot possibly shake hands with them all. [...]

a) Reported rules of British etiquette (geltende gesellschaftliche Umgangsformen; here: use of the instructive expression "be expected to do sth.")
b) The author's comment on the reported personal instructions (see also the use of a concessive clause with "although" and a conditional clause with "unless"; FOR DETAILS, CF. III, 10)

The **personal instructions** that follow are a recommendation of a social rule:

> ⬒ A hostess (['həʊstɪs], Gastgeberin) *should* always shake hands with each of her guests. ⊟ *When* one person is introduced to another they *should* both murmur, "How do you do?"; *never* [*should* they say] "Pleased to meet you" or "Hi" or "Hallo".
> *You do not* shake hands *when* introduced to another person in the street.
> ⬓ Children *should* be taught to shake hands with guests *when* they enter a room to be introduced.
>
> (MARTINE LEGGE, *ETIQUETTE*. LONDON, 1964, P. 46)

⬒ Beginning
a) One of the elements into which a general behavioural concept (Gesamtvorstellung von Verhalten) can be analysed (here: "a hostess" at a party)
b) Instead of imperative sentences, use of recommendations with "should" in the verbal groups

⊟ Middle
c) Further elements, listed in some convincing order (here: from hostess and guests, to guests and guests at a party, in contrast to stranger and stranger "in the street", to "children" and guests)
d) Use of clauses to show the context (Zusammenhang) for which the instructions are intended (here: three time clauses with "when"; CF. II, 2)

⬓ End
e) The most important or the least important element (here: from "hostess" to "children"; in the given text, the least important element)

2) Personal instructions, reported as part of a longer text interpretation:
– The framing part of the **text interpretation** might take the following form:

> ...Obviously, the most striking aspect of the dialogue in Pinter's sketch ["Request Stop"] is the fact that the WOMAN never gets any answers from

those she speaks to. ▭ *To be able to understand* some of the reasons that may explain such behaviour, *we may draw on* (zurückgreifen auf) the "conversational maxims" (Grundsätze) that have been listed by Willis Edmondson and Juliane House.

▭ Beginning
a) Use of a linking introduction for the reported instructions (here: "To be able to understand..., we may draw on...")
b) The general behavioural concept (here: "conversational maxims")

– The **personal instructions,** i.e. conversational maxims, may be reported like this:

In their book "Let's talk and talk about it" (München, 1981), Edmondson and House consider *the following maxims* as a basic prerequisite ([ˌpri:ˈrekwɪzɪt], Vorbedingung) of being able to speak English:

c) Brief identification of the source (Quelle) of the reported instructions
d) Repetition, if necessary, of the general behavioural concept (here: "the following maxims")

▭ 1. *You should* support (unterstützen) your hearer ([Zu]Hörer) in a conversation.
2. You *should* avoid anything by which you might give offence (Anstoß erregen).
3. When you want something from your hearer, you *should* give reasons for the requests (Bitten) you make and offer something in return.
4. You *should* be generous (großzügig) in giving information about yourself if your hearer requests (erbitten) such.
5. When you can, you *should* support your hearer when his turn to speak has come.
6. You *should* fill up any conversational gaps (Lücken).
▭ 7. When you receive a social benefit (Nutzen), you *are expected to* give one back.

(Cf. Edmondson and House, p. 47)

▭ Middle
e) For a greater number of instructions: use of a listing order with ordinal numbers (Ordnungszahlen) to introduce each of the elements into which the general behavioural concept has been analysed (here: 1., 2., etc. up to 7.)
f) To report imperative sentences ("Support your hearer..."), "should" is used (here: "You should support", etc.)
g) Use of the second-person pronoun "you" to name the receiver (Empfänger) of the instructions (here: "you" in a possible situation for the expected behaviour)
h) Use of clauses to show the context in which the instructions apply (zur Anwendung kommen) (here: "by which you" [2], "when you" [3], "when you can", etc.)

▭ End
i) The most important or the least important element (here: from the most general and most important maxim in 1. to the least important in the list, see 7.)

– The frame of the **text interpretation** may be taken up again like this:

Reading *these maxims,* we will immediately realise how many of them are flouted (mißachten) both by THE OTHERS and the WOMAN. Right at the beginning of the conversation, the other person at the bus stop, a SMALL MAN,...

j) Re-introduction (Wiedereinführung) of the general behavioural concept as a long-distance signal (Fernsignal) (here: "these maxims")

3) **Practical instruction,** from a handbook for writers of research papers (wissenschaftliche Abhandlungen):

[...]

▭ 2.6 Quotations

2.6.1 Use of quotations

While quotations (Zitate) are a common and often effective feature (Kennzeichen) of a research paper, ⊟ *use* them selectively (auswählend). *Quote* only words, phrases, lines, and passages that are particularly interesting, vivid (lebendig), unique (einzigartig), or apt (passend), and *keep* all quotations as brief as possible. Overquotation *can bore* (langweilen) *your* readers and *might lead* them to conclude that you are neither an original thinker nor a skillful writer.

In general, a quotation – whether a word, phrase, sentence, or more – *should* correspond (entsprechen) exactly to its source (Quelle) in spelling, capitalization (Großschreibung), and interior punctuation (Zeichensetzung im Text). *If* you change it in any way, *make* the alteration (Abänderung) *clear* to the reader, following *the rules and recommendations* explained below.

2.6.2 Prose

Unless special emphasis (Nachdruck) *is required* (erforderlich sein), prose quotations of not more than four type lines *should* be placed in quotation marks and incorporated within (aufnehmen in) the text.

▭ Beginning

a) A general behavioural concept (here: use of "quotations" in a research paper)

b) For a great number of instructive sentences, paragraphs, or sections, use of a listing order with ordinal numbers to introduce each of the elements into which the general concept has been analysed (here: "2.6" and "2.6.1", "2.6.2")

⊟ Middle

c) Use of simple imperative sentences in impersonal practical instruction (here: "use", "quote", etc.)

d) Imperative sentences may be replaced by statements (Aussagesätze) which show what *can, may,* or *might* happen if the instruction is not followed (here: "Overquotation *can* bore your readers...", etc.)

e) Instead of imperative sentences, verbal groups with "should" may be used

f) Use of clauses to show the context for which the instruction may apply (here: a conditional clause, "If you change...", etc.)

g) From time to time, use of sentences with instructive expressions instead of imperative clauses (here: "is required", "need not" [brauchst nicht], "you may want to" [wohlberaten sein zu])

"It was the best of times, it was the worst of times," wrote Charles Dickens of the eighteenth century.

Remember, though, that *you need not* always reproduce (wiedergeben) complete sentences. Sometimes *you may want to* quote just a word or phrase as part of your sentence.

For Charles Dickens the eighteenth century was "the best of times" and "the worst of times."

☐ *You may put* a quotation at the beginning, middle, or end of your sentence or, for the sake of (um … willen) variety (Abwechslung) or better style, *divide* it by your own words.

[…]

(JOSEPH GIBALDI AND WALTER S. ACHTERT, *MLA HANDBOOK FOR WRITERS OF RESEARCH PAPERS.* NEW YORK: THE MODERN LANGUAGE ASSOCIATION OF AMERICA, 1984, P. 48.)

☐ End
h) A final, more general instruction

4) **Statutory instruction,** from the regulations of the British "Highway Code":

75. *Drive* at a steady (gleichmäßig) cruising speed (Reisegeschwindigkeit) comfortably within *your* capacity (Leistungsvermögen) and that of your vehicle.

a) Use of a listing order with ordinal numbers to introduce each rule or regulation separately (getrennt)
b) Use of simple imperative sentences

Lane discipline

76. *After* entering the left-hand traffic lane (Fahrbahn) of a motorway, stay in it long enough to accustom yourself to (sich gewöhnen an) the speed of vehicles in that lane *before* attempting to move out into a faster right-hand lane to overtake.

c) Use of clauses to show the context for which the instruction applies (here: temporal clauses: "After entering…", "before attempting…"

77. KEEP WITHIN THE CARRIAGEWAY LANE MARKINGS (Markierungen der Fahrbahnspur), *cross* them only when changing from one lane to another. *Before* changing lanes *be sure* that it is safe to do so, par-

ticularly at high speeds. <u>DO NOT WANDER FROM LANE TO LANE.</u>

(Cf. *The Highway Code*, London: HMSO, 1968, pp. 16 f.)

d) Use of "do" in negative imperative sentences (here: "Do not wander from..."), with emphasis given by capitalization and underlining to the most important instruction

5) **Statutory instruction,** from "The Queen's Regulations for the Royal Air Force" (4th edition) on how to treat prisoners of war:

SECT. 6.–PRISONERS OF WAR:

▭ **J 917. Responsibility for Prisoners of War.**

▤ 1) Both the Government whose forces capture them and the individual members of those forces *are responsible* (verantwortlich) *for ensuring* (sicherstellen) *that,* from the moment of capture, prisoners of war are treated *in accordance with the requirements of* the Geneva Convention Relative to (mit Bezug auf) the Treatment of Prisoners of War 1949.

2) Prisoners *are* on no account (auf keinen Fall) *to* be regarded as the property (Eigentum) of or at the mercy of (ausgeliefert sein) the units or individuals who capture them or have them in their charge (Obhut). ▢ Consequently all persons who have prisoners of war in their charge *are* strictly *to* observe in their treatment of them the requirements of the Geneva Convention of 1949...

(Amendment List No. 59; Ministry of Defence, January 1971; HMSO)

▭ Beginning

a) A general behavioural concept (here: "Responsibility for Prisoners of War")

▤ Middle

b) Use of a listing order to enumerate (aufzählen) each of the elements into which the general behavioural concept has been analysed (here: [1], [2]...)

c) Use of instructive expressions which refer to moral or statutory (gesetzlich) principles (here: "are responsible for ensuring that", "in accordance with the requirements of")

d) Instead of imperative sentences, use of the forms of "be to" (sollen, auf Anordnung oder nach Vereinbarung) (here: "are on no account to be regarded as", "are strictly to observe")

▢ End

e) The last element of the analysed behavioural concept

6) **Statutory instruction,** sections of "Article I" of the U.S. Constitution (1787)

ARTICLE I

Sec. 1. All legislative powers herein granted *shall* be vested in (als Recht übertragen werden auf) a Congress of the United States, which *shall* consist of a Senate and House of Representatives.

Sec. 2. The House of Representatives *shall* be composed of members chosen every second year by the people of the several states [...].

In legally binding statutory instruction, replacement (Ersatz) of imperative sentences by statements with the auxiliary "shall" (soll, sollen) in the verb group (here: "shall be vested in", "shall consist of", etc.) Use of "shall" to express what must be done because some lawmaking authority says so.

7) **Reported statutory instruction,** here concerning rulings (Entscheide) of U.S. federal courts (bundesstaatliche Gerichte)

▀ The federal courts consistently (konsequent) *upheld* (bestätigen, stützen) the treaties made with Indian tribes ▬ and also *held* that property *may not* be taken from Indians, whether or not a treaty exists, "except in fair trade." The latter contention (Ansicht) was offered by the Hualapai Indians against the Santa Fe railway. The company *was required by the courts* in 1944 to relinquish (abtreten) about 500,000 acres it thought *had been granted to* it by the U.S. The lands had been occupied since prehistory by the Indians, without benefit of (ohne die Vorteile von) treaty recognition (Anerkennung), and ▄ the Supreme Court *held* that, if the occupancy (Wohndauer) could be proved, as it subsequently (anschließend) was, the Indians *were entitled to* have their lands restored (zurückerstatten). [...]

(*Encyclopaedia Britannica*, 1975, vol. 13, p.222)

▀ Beginning
a) In narrative texts, report of the statutory instruction in the past tense group if it belongs to the past (here: "upheld", "held")
b) A general behavioural concept (here: "the treaties made with Indian tribes")

▬ Middle
c) Use of instructive expressions to sum up and report the rulings or regulations (here: "to uphold sth.", "to hold that", "may not", "be required to", "be granted to", "be entitled to")
d) Dates or years to show when the reported statutory instruction was passed (verabschieden; here: "in 1944")

▄ End
e) The last element or the latest (neuest) development

General steps for writing or reporting an instructive text

1) Use an introduction with the **general behavioural concept** which you want to analyse into **elements** for instructions.
If you report instructions, use a **linking introduction** (verknüpfende Einleitung) for the reported instructions.
A linking introduction incorporated (aufnehmen) into a text interpretation may read like this:

> ... To be able to *understand* some of the reasons that *may explain* such behaviour, we may draw on the "conversational maxims" that have been listed by Willis Edmondson and Juliane House.

The general behavioural concept may then be introduced in this way:

> In their book "Let's talk and talk about it" (München, 1981), Edmondson and House consider the following *maxims as a basic prerequisite of being able to speak English: ...*

2) When reporting **statutory instruction,** identify (if possible) the title, year and legislative body (gesetzgebende Institution) by which it was issued.

> Article I of the U.S. *Constitution* of *1787* refers to the "legislative powers" of the U.S. federal government. It lays down that Congress shall consist of two chambers (Kammern), the House of Representatives and the Senate.
> (Or: *The thirteen signatory states* laid down that Congress should / was to consist of two chambers,...)

*

3) After your introduction, continue with a **listing order** to name each of the **elements** into which you have analysed the general behavioural concept.
For short **personal instructions,** you can often do without listing numbers. For a greater number of instructions, however, use a listing order with ordinal numbers (Ordnungszahlen).
Arrange the list of instructions according to a recognisable (erkennbar) principle: from important to less important, from less important to important, from general to particular (or vice versa [umgekehrt]).

> [...]
> *1.* You should support your hearer in a conversation.
> *2.* You should avoid anything by which you might give offence.
> *3.* ...

4) Write instructive sentences in accordance with the kind of instructive text form in which they appear.
a) In **personal instructions** addressed to others, use "should" in the verbal groups and **polite forms of instructive expressions** ("Could / Would you do X", "I would like you to do X", etc.; (CF. "TEXT FORM DICTIONARY", III, 12, I).

> A hostess *should* always shake hands with each of her guests. When one person is introduced to another they *should* both murmur, "How do you do?"...

When using imperative sentences in personal instructions from one person to another, add "Please".

> *Please, hand* in your typed copies by Friday, 1 June. The first page *should* give your name, your instructor's name, the course number, and the date in separate lines...

b) In impersonal **practical instruction,** you can use **imperative sentences** and sentences with the auxiliaries "have to" or "must" in verbal groups, giving reasons where possible. For variety (Abwechslung), you can also use **instructive expressions** of the type "You are expected/intended to do X" (CF. "TEXT FORM DICTIONARY", III, 12, II).

> ...*keep* all quotations as brief as possible. Overquotation *can bore* (langweilen) your readers and *might lead* them to conclude that...

c) In **reported statutory instruction,** you can use the following forms:
– the auxiliaries "be to" or "shall" as in the original instruction when writing in the present tense:

> "The Queen's Regulations for the Royal Air Force" of 1971 *say* that prisoners *are* on no account *to* be regarded as the property of or at the mercy of the units or individuals who capture them...
>
> According to the U.S. Constitution of 1787, the legislative powers *shall be* vested in two chambers...

– **summary** (zusammenfassend) **instructive expressions** like "to rule" (vorschreiben), "to demand" (fordern), "to prohibit", etc. (CF. "TEXT FORM DICTIONARY", III, 12, III).

> The federal courts consistently *upheld* the treaties made with Indian tribes and also *held* that property *may not* be taken from Indians whether or not a treaty exists...

– the tenses of the past tense group (CF. II, 2) for reporting statutory instruction if it is no longer accepted or is closely linked with past events:

> ...the Supreme Court *held* that, if the occupancy (Wohndauer) [of an Indian tribe in one area] could be proved [...], the Indians *were entitled* to have their lands restored.

If you report statutory instruction that is still accepted, or look at it from the point of view of what the text, though written in the past, still says when read today, you use the tenses of the present tense group (CF. II, 2).

> In 1929 a [...] Geneva convention [...] made provision for (bestimmen) the protection of prisoners of war [...], providing (vorsehen) that belligerents ([bɪ'lɪdʒərənts], kriegführende Länder) *must treat* prisoners humanely (menschenwürdig), *supply* (liefern) information about them, and *permit* visits to prison camps by representatives of neutral states.

5) Use **clauses (of time, place, condition, manner)** to show the context (Zusammenhang) in which the instructions apply (gelten, zur Anwendung kommen). The time clauses may be shortened by a participle, as in this example:

> 76. *After* enter*ing* the left-hand traffic lane of a motorway, *stay* in it long enough to accustom yourself to the speed of vehicles in that lane *before* attempt*ing* to move out into a faster right-hand lane to overtake.

6) Use **adverbs of manner** ending in -ly (Adverbien der Art und Weise) if you have to characterize the planned behaviour more precisely.

> In general, a quotation – whether a word, phrase, sentence, or more – should correspond *exactly* to its source in spelling, capitalization, and interior punctuation.

(CF. "TEXT FORM DICTIONARY", III, 12.)

Some areas of use

The shorter kinds of instructive text form are often used:

a) as **recommendations** (Empfehlungen) for action or changes when added to a comment (CF. II, 10). An instructive sentence or paragraph usually forms the conclusion, for instance, to a **leading article.**

> ... At some point in the next few weeks the Cabinet may be forced to choose between supporting the Prime Minister and risking the break-up of the Commonwealth. *If she is wise, Mrs Thatcher will draw back* before obliging her colleagues to make such a choice.
>
> ("AFRICA WANTS SANCTIONS NOT CROCODILE TEARS", IN: *THE OBSERVER*, 13 JULY 1986, P. 10)

b) as **reported** plans, rules, regulations, or acts of legislative bodies, incorporated (aufnehmen, einbauen), for instance, into **historical narration** (CF. II, 3) or into a **text interpretation** (CF. II, 9).

> The High Court (Oberstes Gericht), called upon (anrufen) last week to balance (abwägen) the competing (im Wettstreit liegen, gegensätzlich) public interests of free speech and protecting the secrecy (['si:krəsɪ], Verschwiegenheit) of MI5 (englischer Geheimdienst), tied itself in knots and left Kafkaesque gags (Knebel, Mundsperre) on "The Observer" and the "Guardian".

A first sentence with **reported statutory instruction** then follows:

> As a result, we *may not* repeat a report we carried on 22 June about the British Government's attempt to stop a former (früherer) British agent, Mr Peter Wright, publishing his memoirs in Australia.

A passage of narration divides this sentence off from another passage of reported statutory instruction:

> We revealed then that his book contains evidence of criminal acts committed (begangen) by MI5 between 10 and 30 years ago and briefly described them. The "Guardian" carried (bringen, veröffentlichen) a similar article the following day.

Then a second passage of **reported statutory instruction** follows:

> We *are not allowed to* tell you precisely what we said three weeks ago, even though newspapers as diverse (verschiedenartig) as "The Times", "El Pais" and "Pravda" are perfectly at liberty (völlig frei sein) to tell *their* readers. What is more (Darüber hinaus), if they or any other news organisation at home or abroad (im Ausland), reveals fresh information about the contents of the Wright memoirs, "The Observer" and the "Guardian" alone *are prevented from* (werden daran gehindert) carrying that information.

A comment, with a **summary instructive expression,** concludes the text:

> These absurd and illogical *restrictions* (Beschränkungen) remain, though no evidence was produced in the High Court that we or the "Guardian" have harmed (verletzen) national security or that we were about to do so. This is not just another instance of the law proving itself an ass (Esel). It is an attempt (Versuch) by the State to use the courts to fashion (herstellen, liefern) new weapons of censorship (Zensur).
> ("KAFKA GAG FOR PRESS", IN: *THE OBSERVER*, 13 JULY 1986, P. 10)

c) as part of a **personal letter** or a **formal letter** (such as a business letter in commercial [Handels-] correspondence). In letters generally, we write in accordance with the same rules of good composition as apply (gelten) in the text forms we have studied in this guide.
However, a letter has the following six conventional parts: a *heading* (Briefkopf), with the writer's address and the date; the *inside address* (Empfängeranschrift); the *salutation* (Anrede); the *body* (Text, Hauptteil); the *complimentary close* (Schlußformel); and the writer's *signature* (Unterschrift). The personal letter has the same parts, except the inside address:

```
          Hebbelstr. 9
          1000 Berlin 33
          W. Germany

          March 11, 19..

The Bookseller's Corner
High Street
Oxford
England

Dear Sirs,

I thank you very much for
sending me your catalogue
of books in print, 19... I
would like to order the fol-
lowing titles:

1. John Ardagh, Germany
   and the Germans (Hamish
   Hamilton)
2. Frances FitzGerald,
   Cities on a Hill (Pica-
   dor)
3. R. W. Holder, A Diction-
   ary of American and
   British Euphemisms
   (Bath UP)
```

a) *The heading:* writer's address, followed by the date

b) *Inside address:* not used in a personal letter

c) *Salutation:* the first word and all nouns are capitalized ("Dear Madam", "Dear Mr. Lee"). In the U.S., the salutation is followed by a colon (Doppelpunkt) in formal letters

d) The *body* of the letter; here: personal instructions. Use of polite style 1) by addressing the instructions to the writer ("I would like to"), 2) by instructive expressions for politeness ("Please let me know", "you may add")

Please let me know whether the following title, which I find in your catalogue of 1980, is still available:

> Hugh Cudlipp, The Prerogative of the Harlot: Press Barons & Power (The Bodley Head)

If you should have this book in stock, you may add it to my present order.

Payment will be made by Eurocheque as soon as I receive your invoice.

Yours faithfully,

(Miss) Annette Marbert

e) *Complimentary close:* in formal letters also used: "Yours respectfully,"; in personal letters: "Yours sincerely", "Sincerely", "Cordially", etc.
f) *Signature:* handwritten under the complimentary close. In a typewritten letter, the name of the writer is typed under the signature

Part III

Text form dictionary

1. Impressionistic and technical descriptions

Talking about a descriptive text

to give a description of...

to convey (vermitteln)	a picture an impression	of (a setting / scene / situation / ...)

to give a description with attention to (Blick für) the	detail atmosphere local colour characteristics	of...

to give a(n)	accurate (treffend) faithful (wahrheitsgetreu) detailed	description of...

this	paragraph scene text	gives a	lively(['laɪvlɪ],lebendig) vivid (lebensecht) lifelike broad (allgemein) rough ([rʌf], grob)	description of...

the	description colourful adjectives comparisons (Vergleiche) images (Bilder) metaphors picturesque language	create(s) an atmosphere of (danger / ...) portray(s) (ausmalen) the local colour of... evoke(s) (heraufbeschwören) a suggestion / tone of...

to describe the room / house in which (*X* lives / ...)

to	describe sketch	the	scene where... setting where...

to describe the	scenery (Landschaft) of... environment (Umgebung) of... natural surroundings of... panorama of... vista (Aus-/Fernblick) that presents itself (sich eröffnen) from...

to portray (schildern, darstellen) aspects of...

I. Describing a picture

The beginning of your description of a picture

The	situation	is	at... (a place)
	scene		near...

The scene / picture introduces	us	to...
	the viewer (Betrachter)	
	the spectator	

In the / this	picture	we	see...
	photo		come upon (stoßen auf)...
	painting		catch a glimpse (flüchtiger Eindruck) of...
	cartoon		
	illustration		

We / The viewer come(s) upon a	strange	sight (Anblick) of...
	unusual	view (Ansicht) of...
	beautiful	

The picture	gives	a view	of...
	presents	a glimpse	
	conveys		

For the middle of your description of a picture

In the foreground	there is / are...
On the left	
In the front on the left (Im Vordergrund links)	

In the foreground we	can see...
	come in sight of (erblicken)...
	catch sight of...
	get a (good /...) view of...
	have a (fine / shocking / depressing /...) view of...

In the middleground of	the picture	is / are...
In the centre of	the scene	there is / are...

On the right	there is / are...
In the front on the right (Im Vordergrund rechts)	

The	picture	is dominated (wird beherrscht) by	two	groups of	people
	scene		three		objects
			...		elements

The group	on the left	is standing (at / next to / near / ...)
	in the middle	moves (towards / in the direction of / ...)
	on the right	looks (at / up to / down from / ...)

Behind (Hinter)	*A*	we see	*B*
In front of (Vor)		there is	
To the back of		there goes (bewegt sich)	
To the right of (Rechts von)		runs	

For the end of your description of a picture

In the background there is / are...
From left to right there is / are...
From below to above (Von unten nach oben) the picture is dominated by...

The general impression we / the viewer get(s) is one of	peaceful togetherness
	violent uproar

II. Giving an impressionistic description of a place or person

For the beginning of an impressionistic description

Before me I	see	a	beautiful	sight (Anblick)	of...
	saw		grand (großartig)	spectacle (Schauspiel)	
	had		ghastly (grauenerregend)	scene	

It is a scene of (great / ...) beauty when...
Here in *X* (place name) all is (quiet / ...)

X (person's name) could be	described	as (a man / woman of...)
	characterized	as...

s/he	looks younger / older than...
	presents himself / herself as...
	impresses himself / herself as...

X (a place / house / building / room) lies	in the centre of...
	at the foot of (a hill / mountain)

X looks	on to (geht hinaus auf) (a garden / park / lake / …)
	out over (a lake)
	out at (a place)
	up at (a mountain)
	down (a road)
	down upon (a valley)

Adjacent to (Angrenzend an)	*X* (a building / room / …) there is…
Next to	

X (a place / region) is	ringed (umgeben)	by…
	surrounded (umgeben)	
	bordered (begrenzt)	

X is lined (umgrenzt) with (a row of…)

X	extends (sich ausdehnen)	to…
	stretches (sich erstrecken)	

X lies	in…
	to the north / south / east / west (of…)
	in the north / south / east / west

X (a place / town / region)	contains (enthalten)…
	is crowded with (übervölkert)…
	is covered with (bedeckt) (a layer [Schicht] of…)

X (a place / object) is shaped (geformt) like a…

X is	boat-shaped
	fan-shaped (wie ein Fächer / fächerförmig)
	U-shaped / T-shaped / V-shaped / Y-shaped / …

X looks like a…

X looks	as if he/she/it	were…
		wanted (möchte) to…

For the middle of an impressionistic description

Here At this end Here, at this end,	you have… you can see… (there) lies… (there) stands / rises (erhebt sich) / runs (verläuft)… (there) grows…

There At the other end Over there Over there, on the right/left,	you see…

– use of "with" or "without" plus participle

There is / are (also)	some *X*s (persons, animals), some *X*s (objects),	**with** *A* (walk**ing** behind…) **with** *A* (attach**ed** to…)

In a corner In the far corner	there is *Y*,	**without** (ohne daß er/sie) look**ing** at *X* **without anybody** tak**ing** notice of (ohne daß jemand Notiz nimmt von)…

At the edge (Rand) of *X* Along the inner / outer circle (Kreis) On the periphery ([pə'rɪfərɪ], am äußersten Rand)	there is / are…

– use of clauses with "where" or "wherever" (local clauses)

At *X* (a place name), Near *X*,	**where** *Y* meets…, **where** *Y* joins (sich verbindet mit)…, **where** *Y* links up with…,	there is / are…

Wherever (Wohin auch immer) you look, you see (happy faces / …)

X (a person)	is (6 ft. 2 / …) weighs (7 stone / …)

s/he has a	muscular / … build (Körperbau) straight (aufrecht) / … bearing (Haltung) firm (fest) / … gait (Gang)

For the end of an impressionistic description

In the distance (Ferne)	you can see…
On the horizon [hə'raɪzn]	
In the sky (Am Himmel)	
On the surface (Oberfläche)	

On the outer rim (Rand)	you will find…
On the edge	you will come upon (stoßen auf)…
On the borders	there is / are…
Beyond (Jenseits)	

III. Giving a technical description

For the beginning of a technical description

X has the	form	of…
	shape (Gestalt)	
	size (Größe)	
	volume (Umfang, Ausmaß)	
	extension (Ausdehnung)	

X is	circular (kreisrund)
	oval
	rectangular (rechteckig)
	quadrangular ([kwɒ'dræŋgjələ], viereckig)
	angular (eckig)
	triangular (dreieckig)
	five-sided (fünfseitig)

For the middle of a technical description

X measures (mißt) 200 ft. / 10 by 15 ft. / …

X is *n* (a figure [Zahl])	feet	wide (breit)
	yards	long
	centimetres	deep
	metres	high
	miles	
	kilometres	

X weighs *n* (a figure)	pounds
	hundredweights (Zentner)
	tons

X is *n* (a figure)	inches (Zoll) centimetres feet	thick in diameter ([daɪ'æmɪtə], Durchmesser)

X has a	length height [haɪt] width (Breite) weight [weɪt] thickness	of…

For the end of a technical description

All in all (Insgesamt), there is / are…
To complete (vervollständigen) *X*, there is / are…

2. Stories

Talking about stories

A writer tells a story (in a serious / playful tone)

s/he	narrates ([næ'reɪts], erzählt) tells of	events / incidents (in…)

s/he tells sb. (him / her) about what happened	in (a place) on (a date)

sb. is a	story-teller narrator (Erzähler)

a writer	gives presents	a	chronological detailed lively	account (Darstellung) of what happened

s/he gives a(n)	factual (sachlich) first-hand (aus erster Hand) eye-witness (Augenzeugen-)	account of…

s/he gives a(n)	personal subjective partial (parteiisch) impartial (unparteiisch)	account of…

s/he takes the role of a(n)	observer (Beobachter) onlooker spectator (Zuschauer) story-teller I-narrator (Ich-Erzähler)

The beginning of a story

Once (Einmal, einst) On one occasion (Einmal)	*X* (did *Y*)

Not (so) long ago (Vor nicht langer Zeit), Some time ago Recently (Kürzlich) A little / short while ago	*X* (did *Y* / happened in...)

Originally (Ursprünglich),...

Last	night... week... month... year...

A fortnight ago... The other day (Neulich) The day before yesterday (Vorgestern) Yesterday This morning (Heute morgen) At noon today (Heute mittag) At noontime (mittags)	*X* (happened in...)

At (9 /...) o'clock in the	morning afternoon evening	*X* (did *Y*)

The middle of a story

Then...
Shortly afterwards (Kurz danach)...
A short time afterwards...

After a while (Nach einiger Zeit)...
Later...

And then…
Two minutes (hours / days / …) later…

After that…
Thereafter…
Next (Als nächstes)…

– clauses for the time before sth. happened (time clauses)

Before *X* | did / had done | *Y*, he…

(Two / …) | years / months | **before** *X* did *Y*, he…

By the time (Bis [Zu dem Zeitpunkt, daß]) *X* had (done *Y*), he…

– clauses for what happened at the same time in the past (time clauses)

When (als)
As soon as (Sobald)
As (In dem Augenblick, als) | *X* did *Y*, *Z* happened

While (Während)
As long as (Solange wie)
Until the day that (Bis zu dem Tag, an dem) | *X* did *Y*, *Z* did…

And then…
All at once (Ganz plötzlich)…
Suddenly…
The next moment (Im nächsten Augenblick)…

Immediately afterwards (Sofort danach)…
At once (Sofort)…
That day (An jenem Tag)…
That night…
That evening…

During (Während) the following (ten / …) days…
For the next hour (Die nächste Stunde lang)…
For a week (Eine Woche lang)…
For a fortnight (Vierzehn Tage lang)…

The end of a story

At last ([Doch] Schließlich)...
Eventually (Schließlich, Am Ende)...
In the end (Schließlich)...
Finally (Zum Schluß, Als Letztes)...

<table><tr><td>And to</td><td>top
cap</td><td>it all (Und um das Maß vollzumachen)...</td></tr></table>

3. Reports

Talking about a report

<table><tr><td>A writer</td><td>gives
presents
writes</td><td>a report (on sth.)</td></tr></table>

<table><tr><td>s/he writes a</td><td>sports report
war report
(school) report (Zeugnis)</td></tr></table>

<table><tr><td>s/he reports</td><td>sth. to sb. (him / her)
from (a place)
that sth. (happened in...)</td></tr></table>

<table><tr><td>s/he gives a(n)</td><td>factual
impartial (unparteiisch)
objective</td><td>account of...</td></tr></table>

his/her story (Darstellung) is that...

The beginning of a report

Formerly (Früher)...
In the old days (Früher)...
Around (1600)...
In the year (1620 /...)...
In 45 B.C. (vor Christus)...
In 9 A.D. (nach Christus)...
On 4 July 1776...

At the beginning of (the 19th century / ...)...
In the 16th and 17th centuries...

There were (two important / outstanding / ...) events in (1787 / ...) which...
Originally (Ursprünglich)...
At first (Anfangs)...

The middle of a report

Later,...
Later on, in (1791 / ...), ...

A	year	later, ...
	decade (['dekeɪd], Jahrzehnt)	
	century (Jahrhundert)	

During the (19th / ...) century, ...
In the course (Verlauf) of the (20th / ...) century, ...
In the period from (1780 / ...) to (1810 / ...), ...

At the time of	*X*'s reign (Herrschaft)...
At the beginning of	*X*'s rule over...
At the end of	the *X* (Eisenhower / Kennedy / ...) administration...
	the *X* (Wilson / Thatcher / ...) government...

In the interval (Zwischenzeit) between...
Subsequently (Anschließend, In der Folgezeit)...
From that time onwards...

The end of a report

In the end, in (1814 / ...), ...
Eventually (Schließlich), towards the end of (the decade, ... / century, ... / reign of *X*, ...), ...
Finally, in (1918 / ...), ...
By the end (Bis zum Ende) of the war, ...

4. Definitions

Talking about a definition

A writer	gives finds arrives at	a definition of (a word / term [Begriff] / ...)

s/he gives a(n)	clear exact precise narrow (eng) correct broad (weit) wrong incomplete (unvollständig)	definition of

s/he defines a word (term / ...) as...

According to *A* (a person's name), *X*	can be defined as a... may be defined by the following characteristics

X is defined by the following	aspects distinctive features (unterscheidende Merkmale) criteria ([kraɪ'ti:rɪə], Merkmale, Kriterien)

By *X* the writer	means a... (Unter *X* versteht der Schreiber) means that... understands a... understands that...

In the writer's understanding, the term *X* denotes (bezeichnet) a kind of...
To him/her the term *X* ("flag" / ...) connotes (läßt als Bedeutung mitschwingen) (love of one's country / ...)

The beginning of a definition

To give a definition of To define more precisely	what I/we mean by *X*, I/we want to...

To define what is meant by *X*, I/we can take an example from...
To explain what the word *X* means, we can look at (lines... on page...)

To | explain | our idea of *X*, we can quote (zitieren) *A*, who says...
| clarify (klären) | our concept of *X*, we may draw upon an example from...

I understand *X* to mean a form of *Y* | which...
| by which...
| in which...

Speaking of | *X* (Wenn wir von... sprechen), we mean...
Talking of |
Referring to |

To distinguish between *X* and *Y*, we can...

To make a | nice | distinction (Unterscheidung) between *X* and *Y*, we can say...
| fine |
| first |

When making a comparison between *X* and *Y*, | we see that *X* is a...
Comparing *X* and *Y* |

To explain *X*, | we can draw a parallel to *Y*
To define *X*, | we can draw an analogy to...

X | has...
| contains (enthält)...
| consists of (besteht aus)...
| is composed of (aufgebaut aus)...

X is the kind of *Y* | which...
| by which...

The middle of a definition

Another way of putting it (Anders ausgedrückt), is to speak of...

In other words (Mit anderen Worten), the writer means that...
..., that is to say (das heißt), ...
..., that is (das heißt), ...
Put more simply (Einfacher gesagt), s/he is saying that...
Broadly defined, *X* is a..., i.e. ([aɪ'i:], das heißt) a kind of...

Technically speaking (Fachsprachlich ausgedrückt), Scientifically speaking (Wissenschaftlich ausgedrückt), Politically (Politisch gesehen),	this means…

According to experts on *X*, we can say that… If we go by the experts (Wenn wir uns nach den Experten richten), If we go by an expert on *X* such as *A*,	*Y* can be defined as…

The end of a definition

So we can say that *X*	is… means…

That is one way of defining *X*, namely as…

That is a	minimal broad (grob) wide	definition of what we understand by *X*

5. Explications

Talking about an explication

A writer	gives presents writes	an explication of (a short story / text / paragraph from…)

s/he	explains explicates (fml., erläutern)	in detail the concept ([allgemeine] Vorstellung) of…

s/he	says states	in explicit (klar und deutlich) terms what we understand by…

The beginning of an explication

X (literature / energy / …) can be explained	in two steps in two different ways in one of two ways

X can be	dealt with (behandeln) considered (betrachten) approached (angehen, sich nähern)	from (two / three…) angles (Blickwinkeln) from different points of view

The middle of an explication

The first step	of explaining *X* is to…
One way	
The one way	

From the first	angle	*X*	is…
	point of view		has…
			consists of…
			is made of…
			refers to (bezieht sich auf)…

The second step	is to…
Another (ein weiterer) way	
A further way	

The	other	way of explaining *X* refers to… /proceeds by…
	second	

The	first	element is the fact that…
	second	
	third	

Moreover (Darüber hinaus),	we have to consider that…
Furthermore (Weiterhin),	we have to take into consideration that…
Besides (Außerdem),	we have to bear in mind (bedenken) that…
In addition (Ferner),	

An example would be…
Another instance of this is…
For example: …
Y, for example, shows that…
In (a country's name), e.g. ([i:'dʒi:], for example) in (the region of…), …

Especially,	if we think of…
Particularly (Besonders),	
In particular (Insbesondere),	

…, in other words (anders gesagt), *X*	is…
…, that is, *X*	refers to…
…, that is to say (das heißt), *X*	

X can be explained as..., namely as a kind of...
..., or rather (oder besser [gesagt]), *X* has...

Also (Ferner), Similarly (Ähnlich), Equally (Ebenfalls), Likewise (Gleichfalls),	it is true (trifft es zu) to say that *X* is / has...

The end of an explication

So As a result, All in all (Insgesamt gesehen), By and large (Im großen und ganzen),	we can say that...

Altogether (Insgesamt), In short (Kurz gesagt), Briefly (Kurz [gesagt]), In one word, In a word (Mit einem Wort), In brief (In aller Kürze),	there is / are... *X* is...

To sum up, Summing up, In sum (Zusammengefaßt),	*X* is / has...

The	third last final	aspect is...

The (third / ...) and last element is...

And thirdly, *X* has...
Lastly, ...

Finally, *X* can be viewed (betrachten) as composed of...

6. Outlines

Talking about a topic outline

A writer	makes gives writes	a(n)	outline (Gliederung) word outline topic outline sentence outline

s/he makes a topic outline for a(n)	essay on… paper (Abhandlung, Aufsatz) on… report on…

s/he gives a	brief (knapp) short preliminary ([prɪ'lɪmɪnərɪ], vorläufig) provisional (vorläufig) working (Arbeits-)	outline of…

s/he	outlines the contents of… gives the main headings (Überschriften) of… uses his/her topic outline as a table of contents (Inhaltsverzeichnis)

The beginning of a topic outline

First,…
Firstly,…

1\. …
1.1 …
1.2 …

I. …
    A. …
        1. …
        2. …
    B. …
        1. …
            a. …
            b. …
        2. …
        (etc.)

The middle of a topic outline

Second, . . .
Secondly, . . .

2. . . .
2.1 . . .
2.2 . . .

II. . . .
  A. . . .
  B. . . .
  (etc.)

The end of a topic outline

And (fifth / . . .), . . .
And (fifthly / . . .), . . .

5. . . .
5.1 . . .
5.1.1 . . .
5.1.2 . . .
5.2 . . .
(etc.)

V. . . .
(etc.)

7. Summaries

Talking about a summary

A writer	gives presents writes	a summary of (a text / story / comment / report / ...)

s/he	sums up summarizes	the contents of (a speech / newspaper article / ...) the main ideas of (a text / ...)

The beginning of a summary

To sum up, ...
To summarize, ...
In sum, ...

In brief, ...
In short, ...

To put it briefly, ...
To put it in a nutshell, ... (Um es kurz und bündig zu sagen)

In	simple words, ... simpler terms, ...

Put simply, ... (Einfach gesagt)
Put more simply, ...

The middle of a summary

In his	text, story "..." (title), report on "...",	*X* (name of the writer) speaks of (an event / incident in ... [a place])

In his article, *X*	claims that... argues that... explains how... demands that...

The writer	opens with...	
	introduces his text (story / ...) with...	

s/he deals with *Y* in (three / ...)	steps
	subdivisions

s/he	presents	(three / ...) main arguments in support of...	
	considers	(four / ...) aspects of...	
	distinguishes	(four / ...) elements in...	
	lists (five / ...)	demands	for dealing with *Y*
		principles (Prinzipien)	
		maxims (Grundsätze)	

The end of a summary

The writer closes his text (story / ...) with...

In his concluding (paragraphs / sentences / ...),	the writer	refers to...
At the end,		speaks about...

8. Summarizing minutes

Talking about summarizing minutes

Someone	writes	the minutes (das Protokoll)
	keeps	
	takes	
	reads	

the (minutes) secretary (Protokollant) signs the minutes of... (a discussion)
X (the secretary) minuted (['mɪnɪtɪd], protokollierte) that...

the listeners take the minutes as read (annehmen, wie verlesen)

the minutes of (a date) are	passed (verabschieden)	by (the chairman)
	signed	
	dated	

sb. checks up on (überprüfen) the minutes
s/he circulates (verteilen) the minutes (to members)
s/he questions (in Frage stellen) the minutes as a record (['rekəd], Aufzeichnung) of what was (actually) said
sb. signs the minutes as correct

The beginning of summarizing minutes

The discussion deals with	the following topics...
	(five /...) topics

The following	topics are	discussed
	aspects were	

Only (two /...) topics are dealt with	in detail: Firstly, ... / Secondly, ...
	in some detail:...
	in greater detail:...

In our last (lesson / discussion /...), we talked about the following (three /...) topics: One,... Two,... (And) Three...

The middle of summarizing minutes

The	first	topic	is...
	second		was...
	third		
	...		

As to (Bezüglich)	the first (second / third /...) topic, we said / it was said that...
Concerning	
With regard to (Mit Bezug auf)	

Regarding (Bezüglich) the	question	of *X*, we discussed	first how (why /...)
	problem		secondly, what...
	issue		thirdly, why...

The end of summarizing minutes

The (fifth /...) and last topic we	dealt with	was the question why (how /...)
	considered	

Lastly,	the question was raised whether (ob)...
Finally,	
At the end,	

9. Text interpretations

Talking about a text interpretation

Someone gives an interpretation (Auslegung, Deutung) of a (text / poem / play / novel / difficult paragraph / ...)

s/he	presents writes	a piece of literary criticism on (a novel / ...) an appreciation ([əpri:ʃɪ'eɪʃən], Würdigung) of (a poem / ...)

an interpretation	shows explains elucidates (erhellen) throws light on (beleuchtet)	the meaning of a (text / ...) the significance (Aussage) of a (passage / ...)

a writer	interprets misinterprets (fehlinterpretieren)	a text

s/he engages in an	interpretive discussion on ... interpretive discourse (Interpretationsgespräch) / talk on ...

s/he chooses a particular interpretive approach (Angang, Weg) for dealing with (a text / scene / poem / ...)

The beginning of a text interpretation

The text (story / scene / ...) can be	dealt with explained	from the following points of view

it can be	interpreted elucidated	with the help of the following	concept(s) guiding question(s)

The question concerning (bezüglich) *X*'s text can be	considered approached	from (two / ...) different	angles points of view

The text (article / story / ...) can be	divided into ... subdivided into ... summed up like this

It deals with the following (four / ...) topics: ...

The	writer	asks	the question whether…
	author	raises (aufwerfen)	
		poses (stellen)	

s/he	describes where…
	tells of the time when…
	explains how…
	considers the problem whether…
	deals with the demand to…

(For further details, cf. "Text form dictionary", 1–12.)

The middle of a text interpretation

From the point of view of	the setting,	it is interesting to note that…
	the problem,	
	the thesis,	
	…	

Regarding (In bezug auf)	the question of (setting / plot / metaphor / symbolism /…)
As regards (Was… anbetrifft)	

Concerning the concept of (character /…), we can start from the question how… / who…

Concerning the first (second / third /…) topic,	the	text	says that…
		writer	
		author	
	we can infer (schließen) that…		

With reference to (Mit Bezug auf) *X*, we can quote (zitieren) the following	expressions (on page… / in line…)
	lines (at the top / bottom of page…)
	passage (in / above / below the middle of page…)

To quote a	telling (aufschlußreich)	sentence	from the text: on page… it says (heißt es) that "…"
	relevant	example	

Another (striking /…)	expression	is to be found (findet sich) on page…
	image	
	passage	

The first (second /…)	part subdivision	runs from (geht von)	line… to line… page… to page…

it	describes where… speaks of when… explains how… comments on why…

(For further details, cf. "Text form dictionary", 1–12.)

The end of a text interpretation

So As a result, All in all, Altogether (Insgesamt),	we can say that… the text suggests (legt nahe) that… we see that…

To sum up, In short, In brief	the text (article / scene /…) shows…

Summing up, we can say…

Briefly (Kurz), In a word, In one word, In plain terms, In simple terms,	the writer	shows… illustrates… claims that… comments that… argues that… explains how…

In conclusion, To conclude,	we may say that…

10. Comments

Talking about a comment

A writer makes / gives a comment on sth.
s/he comments on a sentence (view / statement / ...)
s/he comments that...

Outline

I. Expressing one's view
II. Speaking against *A*'s view
III. Choosing between *A*'s and *B*'s view
IV. Solving a problem
V. Trying to persuade somebody
VI. Framing other text forms

I. Expressing one's view

The beginning of a short comment

I | think | that this is not (acceptable / ...)
I | feel | that this is unacceptable (disappointing / ...)
  | would say |
  | would argue (argumentieren) |

I don't think (that) we can | speak of...
  | say that...
  | accept that...

Whether we like it or not, *X* is not *Y*, but *Z*

It seems to me (that) | this is | not the solution (Lösung) to...
  | | not the answer to the problem (of...)
  | | not the answer to the question...

As far as (Soweit) I can see, | this is | not...
  | | unlikely to (wird wahrscheinlich nicht)...

The middle of a short comment

One reason | is that...
  | I would give is...

One argument The first argument	against *A* is that…

Another A second A further	reason argument	is that…

The end of a short comment

So I	would say think don't think would conclude	that…

In short, In brief,	there is nothing to support (stützen) the view (opinion / claim that)…

– use of preposition plus -ing form

This is why (Deshalb) I am opposed **to** accept**ing** (*A*'s view that…)
This is the simple reason why I disagree **with *A*** say**ing** that…

II. Speaking against *A*'s view

The beginning of a comment on someone's view

A	says states (darlegen)	that *X* is a problem

s/he	claims (behaupten) asserts ([ə'sɜ:ts], behaupten)	that	the problem is how to… (wie man… soll) / where to… / when to…

s/he	maintains (behaupten, beteuern) contends (fest behaupten)	that *X* is, I quote, "…"

A	doubts (zweifeln) whether (ob)… casts doubt (zieht in Zweifel) on the fact that… has doubts concerning *X* / as to (bezüglich) how we can…

Contrary to (Im Gegensatz zu) *A*'s view on the subject, *X* is as (good / dangerous /…) as it was (a generation ago / in 1904 /…)

I would like to	question (in Frage stellen)	*A*'s	view that...
	challenge (anfechten)		assertion (Behauptung) that...

As far as (Soweit)	I can see,	*X* is not..., but is...
	I know,	

– use of preposition plus -ing form

Instead of	ask**ing** why...,	I would rather (möchte ich lieber) ask why... / how... / when... / where... / what...
	claim**ing** that...,	
	say**ing** that...,	

The middle of a comment on somebody's view

A's first argument is that...
Firstly, *A* argues that...

However,	*A* does not	see that...
But		acknowledge (anerkennen) that...
		appreciate (würdigen) that...

However, *A* fails (versäumt es) to consider	that...
	why...
	when...
	what...
	under what circumstances...

A is faced with (sieht sich gegenübergestellt)	the difficulty that...
	the question why...
	the problem whether...
	the dilemma that...

For all (Trotz aller)	his arguments in *X*'s support (zur Stützung von),	it seems that there still remains (übrigbleiben) the problem of...
Despite (Trotz) all		we still face the problem how to (wie wir sollen)...

A grounds (gründet) his claim on the	right	premise (Voraussetzung) that...
	wrong	
	false	

– use of preposition plus -ing form

The main reason	**for** not accept**ing** *A*'s first argument is that...
	for say**ing** that... is...

The main reason	**against** *A*'s arguments is that...
	against ***A*** argu**ing** with *X* as evidence is that...

A's second argument is...
Secondly, *A* argues that...

A	uses	the argument	that...
	puts forward (vorbringen)	the idea	
	advances (vorbringen)		
	adduces (fml., anführen)		

A's argument is not objectionable in itself (Für sich genommen, spricht nichts gegen...), but... / yet (doch)...

– preposition plus -ing form

I do not object	**to *A*** argu**ing** (daß *A* argumentiert) that...,	but I	strongly object to the view that...
	to *B* say**ing** that...,		do object to the suggestion that...

I am (seriously / sharply / ...) opposed **to *B*** claim**ing** that...

– use of clauses with "because", etc. (causal clauses)

Since (Da)	*A* limits (begrenzen)	his analysis to...,	few people would accept that...
But **since**	*A* confines ([–'–], beschränken)		
However, **because**			

But *A* is	wrong	to believe that...,	**because**	all the evidence (Beweis[material]) shows that...
	completely wrong		**for** (denn)	

– use of emphasis (Nachdruck)

X is **not** the result (Ergebnis) of..., **but rather** (sondern vielmehr) the work (Einflußnahme) of...

The question is **not** that... / whether...	**What is at issue** (in Frage stehen) is that... The **real** issue (Frage, Problem) is whether...

The end of a comment on somebody's view

So, to my mind, *A*'s	position thesis ['θi:sɪs] solution	is	unconvincing (nicht überzeugend) inconsistent (inkonsequent) inconsistent with (nicht vereinbar) the facts

In sum, *A*'s argument is inconsistent with the evidence advanced by...

There is a contradiction (Widerspruch) between...
The strength of *B*'s argument is that...
Therefore I reject (zurückweisen) the view that...

III. Choosing between *A*'s and *B*'s view

The beginning of a comment on two opposed views

There has been	an argument over a persistent (anhaltend) debate on	what to... (was man... soll) how to...

On one side, there are those who claim that...
On the one hand, there is *A* who asserts that...

On the other side, On the other hand,	there	are those who propose (vorschlagen) to... is *B* who assumes (annehmen) that...

The	question problem issue	is how to...

The middle of a comment on two opposed views

As to (Bezüglich) As for As regards (Was anbetrifft) With reference to (Mit Bezug auf) In regard to Regarding	the claim that...

As to *A*'s assertion (Behauptung), namely that "…" is…

As to the second / *B*'s	claim	that…
	assertion	

B states that "…", and he goes on to say (fährt fort) that "…" [in speech: "quote"… "unquote"]

– use of comparison and comparative clauses

A's view is	similar to	*B*'s in that (dadurch daß)…
	different from	

A's arguments mean very little	compared with (im Vergleich zu)	*B*'s reference to…
	in comparison with	

While *A*	thinks	that…, *B* says…
	holds	
	states	

– use of contrast

A	says	that…,	**whereas** (wohingegen, während [dagegen]) *B* tries to show that…
	concludes (schlußfolgert)		

In contrast to (Im Gegensatz zu)	*A*, *B*	also refers to…
As opposed to		does not mention (erwähnen) that…

By contrast (Dagegen, Im Gegensatz dazu),	*B* quotes (zitieren) *C* as showing that…
Conversely ([kən'vɜ:slɪ], Umgekehrt)	

Contrary to (['kɒntrərɪ], Entgegen) the popular idea (notion [Vorstellung] /…), *B* also claims that…

However (Jedoch),	in *B*'s evidence from…,	there is the flaw (Schönheitsfehler) that…
But		there is a streak (Beimischung) of…
Yet (Doch)		

X, we have to admit (zugeben), is no longer (nicht mehr) only a…. **Rather** (Vielmehr), it is a…

The end of a comment on two opposed views

Considering / Surveying (Wenn wir überblicken) | the conflicting (einander widersprechend) views, I/we (can / have to / ...) come to the conclusion that...

Weighing (Wenn wir abwägen) the pros and cons (das Für und Wider) of the argument, we can conclude (abschließen) by saying (indem wir sagen) that...

As a result (Als Ergebnis), / To conclude, | we may (safely / ...) say that... / we are (fully) justified (können wir mit [vollem] Recht) in saying that...

So, there is nothing very surprising about (*B*'s position / ...). Indeed / In fact (Tatsächlich), there is much to | commend (empfehlen) / recommend | his view that...

– use of preposition plus -ing form

So there is nothing unusual **about** ***B*** | claim**ing** that... / propos**ing** that...

So, on closer inspection (bei genauerem Hinsehen), we may | reach / arrive at / draw | the conclusion that...

IV. Solving a problem

The beginning of a comment on a difficult situation

Concerning (Bezüglich) *X*, it has been | said that... / asked whether...

One | assumption (Annahme) / hypothesis ([haɪˈpɒθɪsɪs], Annahme, Hypothese) | is that...

The | problem / issue | is how to... / what to... / when to...

The (current / ...) | debate / discussion | is whether we (people / ...) should...

– use of quotations (in "…")

The	popular belief common view general opinion notion ([vage] Vorstellung)	is that *X* cannot be changed / solved…

For instance, *A*	says contends (fest behaupten)	that "…"

According to (Nach) *A*, In the words of *A*,	*X* is "…"

A goes on to	say explain argue demand	that "…"

We can also quote *B*, who speaks of "…"
To cite *B* on *X* (Um mit *B* über *X* zu sprechen), "…"

A's	support advocacy (['ædvəkəsɪ], Befürwortung)	of *X* can be summed up like this…

However, it is also	possible permissible (statthaft) admissable (erlaubt) acceptable	to argue that…

Yet (Doch) it is	reasonable (vernünftig) sensible (sinnvoll) appropriate (angemessen)	to say that…

It is (also) possible to	claim doubt (bezweifeln) dispute (in Frage stellen) hypothesize ([haɪ'pɒθɪsaɪz], als Annahme aufstellen)	that it is right (true / correct /…) to say that…

It would be legitimate ([lɪ'dʒɪtɪmɪt], zulässig) for *B* to ask (pose / ...) the question why...

My own opinion / view / thesis / hypothesis is that...

– use of attitudinal adverbs (persuasive style, Stil der Überredung)

It is	surely clearly unquestionably (fraglos)	possible to argue that...

It is	undoubtedly no doubt	legitimate to ask why...

It is obviously (offensichtlich) also correct to claim that...

– use of rhetorical questions (persuasive style)

However, And yet (Und doch),	is this all there is to *X* and to *Y* (mehr hat es nicht mit *X* und *Y* auf sich)?

Given (Vorausgesetzt) all that we have said, should we not...?

However, But	should we not rather (eher, lieber)	look at...? consider the question of...?

– use of viewpoint (Blickwinkel) adverbs

Logically (Logisch gesehen, betrachtet), Politically, though (jedoch), Theoretically, Linguistically (Sprachlich gesehen),	*A*'s position is convincing (right / wrong / silly / ...)

I would (here) like to	give list	(three / ...) arguments against *A*'s contention (Behauptung) that...

I would (also) like to advance (vorbringen) some counter-arguments (Gegenargumente) to *B*'s assertion (Behauptung) that...

I want to present (three / ...) reasons why *A*'s (*B*'s / ...) view of the situation / problem is unacceptable to me

The middle of a comment on a difficult situation

Firstly, I would like to	raise (aufwerfen) pose (vortragen)	the question	whether we can actually say that... whether we really need...

To my mind, *A* does not	give supply (liefern)	conclusive (schlüssig) evidence for his thesis that...

There are a number of foregone ['fɔ:gɒn] conclusions (es steht an vielen Stellen von vornherein fest) in the argument that...

In my view, *A* sidesteps (umgehen) the	problem question issue	of how to... (where to.../...)

Secondly, I would like to draw (your) attention to the fact that *A* does not confront the problem of what to...

Thirdly, And thirdly,	I want to deal more specifically with the problem of how to...

The real problem that *A* faces (gegenüberstehen) is n o t one of... The question is how l o n g ... (when.../...)

It is for this reason (Aus genau diesem Grunde) It is exactly for this reason	that...

As to (Was anbetrifft) my question concerning *X*, I would like to...

– making a concession (Zugeständnis; concessive clauses)

Although ([ɔ:l'ðəʊ], obwohl) **Though**	I (we /...) have to	admit (zugeben) concede ([kən'si:d], einräumen)	that this does not solve the problem of..., I would still (immer noch) argue that...

Although I grant (zugestehen) *A* the point that this Granting that this	does not quite answer the question of... does not fully account for (erklären) the... does not eliminate (ausräumen) the question concerning *X*,	I would still maintain (behaupten) that... I would doubt whether... there must be (serious) doubts whether...

Though many people dismiss (abtun) this	argument perspective (Sicht)	as (unrealistic / idealistic / ...),	I still believe that...

It is true (Zwar) that *A* said (did / ...) *X*. **It is also true** (Es stimmt ferner) that *B* has claimed that... But does this solve the problem of...?

– making conditions for present possibilities (conditional clauses)

If **On condition that** (Unter der Bedingung, daß) **In case** (für den Fall, daß)	*A*	**stopped** saying *X*, **came** to the conclusion that... **were** to give up saying *X*,	we	**would be** able to **might be** able to **might**	solve the problem.

After all (Schließlich), *X* can be considered well accepted by...

Even if (Selbst wenn) my contention (Behauptung)	**is rejected** (zurückweisen), is refuted (widerlegen),	a case **can (could / may / might) be made** (könnte man den Standpunkt vertreten) for...

If **Unless** (Wenn nicht)	*A* accepts that... *A* acknowledges (anerkennen) that...,	(then) the problem **will remain** unsolved (undiscussed /...)

To assume (Anzunehmen) that *X* is *Y*, is an example of arguing	at its most superficial (äußerst oberflächlich) in a circle

– making conditions for past possibilities (conditional clauses)

If this problem **had been considered** before, we **would (should / could / might) have avoided** (vermeiden) the threat of…

We	**might have worked** with…
	could have used…

The end of a comment on a difficult situation

In these circumstances (Unter diesen Umständen),	we have to conclude that…
Within the outlined context (Zusammenhang),	the obvious (offensichtlich) conclusion has to be that…
Against this background,	

In short, (all) the arguments tend to show (weisen stark hin auf) that…

In sum, I/we reach	the (nessessary / inevitable [unausweichlich]) conclusion that…
	the position where we…

In a word, I/we cannot accept	the solution of…
	the suggestion that no solution is possible

So the	consequences (Folgen) of…	support my view that it is right (wrong / inadvisable [nicht ratsam]) to…
	drawbacks to (Nachteile von)…	
	disadvantages of…	
	effects on…	

V. Trying to persuade somebody

The beginning of a strongly persuasive comment

I	fear	that… (*for:* I think / don't think)
	suspect (vermuten, den Verdacht haben)	
	have a hunch (den leisen Verdacht)	

– use of ironical style

What a **marvellous** idea not to…, but to… (*for:* What nonsense)
In *A*'s **remarkable** (bemerkenswert) view I am to blame (tadeln) for saying…
A has **even managed** (hat es sogar fertiggebracht) to reach the **extraordinary** (außerordentlich) conclusion that…
And what **pearls of wisdom** (weise Sprüche) have we got from *A* on…

– use of depreciatory (abwertend) style

Regarding (Bezüglich) *X*, *A* has claimed that....	What a lot of **nonsense!** What a lot of **rubbish!** **Bullshit!**

Concerning young criminals *A* speaks of teenage kids in trouble. *A*'s contention is **a last-ditch attempt** (letzter, verzweifelter Versuch) to postpone (verschieben) reaching the inevitable conclusion (unausweichliche Schlußfolgerung) that...
A seems to **run away from** the conclusion that...
The worst sin (Sünde) in *A*'s argumentation is to speak of...

– use of appreciatory (aufwertend) style

Concerning crimes committed by youths, *A* speaks of young criminals, while to *B* they are just **teenage kids**

The middle of a strongly persuasive comment

– Use of intensifying adverbs

I think it is	completely (völlig) totally utterly (ganz und gar)	wrong to believe, as *A* does, that...

In my opinion, it is	more or less almost (fast) absolutely (völlig)	impossible to...

I think *A*'s	suggestion proposal (Vorschlag)	will prove (wird sich erweisen) hopelessly misconceived (falsch)

A is	seriously thoroughly (['θʌrəlɪ], gründlich) entirely (völlig)	wrong in saying (claiming / ...) that...

He is	badly terribly greatly	mistaken in his conception (Vorstellung, Gedanke) of...

– use of attitudinal adverbs (cf. also III, 10, IV)

Surely, Obviously (Offensichtlich), Doubtless (Ohne Zweifel),	it is wrong to say that . . .

No doubt, Clearly, Evidently (Offensichtlich), Plainly,	there is nothing harmful (schädlich) about (doing *X*...)

Funnily enough (Seltsamerweise), Amazingly (Überraschenderweise), Strangely (Seltsamerweise),	there is no way to do *X* without doing *Y*

Luckily (Glücklicherweise), Fortunately ['fɔ:tʃənətlɪ],	*A* has also asserted (behaupten) that...

Understandably (Verständlicherweise), Naturally, Typically,	*A* goes on to say that...

Unfortunately (Unglücklicherweise), Regrettably (Bedauerlicherweise), Inevitably (Zwangsläufig),	he fails (versäumt es) to acknowledge (anerkennen) that...

– use of style adverbs

Briefly (Kurz [gesagt]), To be brief, Generally, In general,	*A*'s arguments are a lot of rubbish (Quatsch)

Broadly (Grob [gesprochen]), Crudely (Ganz grob), To put it crudely,	*A*'s arguments are nonsense

Honestly (Ehrlich [gesagt]), In all honesty ['ɒnəstɪ], Frankly (Offen [gesagt]), In all frankness, Bluntly (Geradeheraus [gesagt]), To be blunt,	*A*'s suggestions are a lot of crap (*slang for:* nonsense)

– use of emphasis with "it is *X* which/that..."

A claims that... (methods in foreign-language teaching /...) are difficult. I totally disagree. **It is not** the (METHODS /...) **which** are difficult, **but** the subject of (language /...) itself.

–use of emphasis with "what is"

What is difficult is NOT the (METHODS / ...) but the subject of (language itself)
What is absolutely necessary is NOT to concentrate on (individual WORDS in language learning / ...), but on (structures / ...)

– use of emphasis with "do"

To be quite clear on one thing: I **do think** (meine wirklich) that (teaching methods have to change / ...), and **I do think** we need new ideas for the way we (handle them / ...) But all this does NOT mean that we can continue to disregard (mißachten) the (basic elements of language / ...)

– use of serialization (Reihung) for emphasis

A claims that *X* is... But *X* is **not** about ...ing (fighting / defending oneself / ...), **nor** (und auch nicht) is it a question of... (arms / ...), **and least of all** (am allerwenigsten) is it based on the belief that...

It is true that (Zwar, Es stimmt, daß) *A* did *X*. **It is also true that** *A* had said *Y*. **But it is definitely NOT true** to say that...

The end of a strongly persuasive comment

So, believe me, there is (no way of solving this problem other than [auf andere Weise als] by...)
So, don't have any doubts as to who (darüber, wer) is to blame (tadeln)

What I am	saying simply saying	is this (was ich sagen wollte, ist dies)...

Against the outlined background,	it is to fly in the face of the evidence (steht es in krassem Widerspruch zu den Tatsachen) it is to fly in the face of reason (Vernunft) if we don't (accept / follow / ...)

VI. Framing other text forms

The beginning of a comment that frames other text forms (CF. ALSO III, 9)

The	word expression sentence passage third scene	suggests may imply	that...

However, But	from the point of view of..., within the larger context,	this interpretation this reading (Leseweise)	does not	stand. hold. fails to convince.

Yet, viewed from another angle, this reading	does not carry (much) conviction. lacks conviction (mangelt es an Überzeugungskraft).

The middle of a comment that frames other text forms

– using desriptive text forms to present evidence (CF. II, 1 AND III, 1)

Let me briefly	**describe** depict outline	where	the scene is set... the events happened...

– the beginning of the descriptive text division

The	room house building	is lies is situated	at... on... in the middle of...

Front left there is...
Front right there are...

(CF. "TEXT FORM DICTIONARY", 1)

– the closing part of the comment

So we can	conclude that…
	infer ([ɪn'fɜ:], folgern, schließen) that…

– using narrative text forms to present evidence (CF. II, 2–3 AND III, 2–3)

For evidence (Als Beweis, Beleg),	we can	refer to (verweisen auf)…	(what happened/ how *X* came about)
For support,		**tell the story of…**	
For proof			

– the beginning of the narrative text division

At the beginning,	*X* did *Y*…
At first (Anfangs),	
Then, in 19..,	
Later,	
Several years later,	

Finally, in 19.., *X* had done…
In the end (Schließlich), they…

(CF. "TEXT FORM DICTIONARY 2–3")

– the closing part of the comment

The	story	of what happened…	in…	implies that…
	history		from… to…	means that…
			at the time of…	

– using expository text forms to present evidence (CF. II, 4–9 AND III, 4–9)

One reason is how *A*	**understands**	the term *X*
	defines	the expression *X*
	explains	
	interprets	

– the beginning of the expository text division

For example, *A* speaks of…

Similarly (Ähnlich),	he uses…
Likewise (Ebenso),	

Moreover, according to (nach) *A*, *X*	consists of…
	is composed of…

(CF. "TEXT FORM DICTIONARY", 4–9.)

– *the closing part of the comment*

I have	mentioned cited quoted	these definitions *A*'s explanation of *X*...	to support by (indisputable) evidence the argument that... the thesis that...

– using instructive text forms to present evidence (CF. II, 12 AND III, 12)

The conclusion to be drawn can be summed up by the question of **what should be** (ought to be / ...) **done**

– *the beginning of the instructive text division*

First, we must	review (überprüfen) the notion that... revise (überarbeiten) the view that...

Secondly, we	should have to	(put more effort [Anstrengung] into ensuring [sicherzustellen] that...)

Thirdly (and lastly),	*X* requires (erfordert) a (combined effort to / ...) *X* needs all our strength to...

– *the closing part of the comment*

Unless these	steps suggestions demands	are taken up, are put into practice,	we cannot (achieve [erreichen] our aim to / ...) a solution will not (come in sight / ...)

11. Formal argumentation

Talking about formal argumentation

A writer	argues (argumentieren)	in a scholarly (wissenschaftlich) publication that...

s/he writes a	paper (wissenschaftlicher Aufsatz) research paper (Forschungsarbeit) treatise (Abhandlung)	on...

s/he	writes a term paper ([Schüler-]Referat) presents a piece of formal (scientific [nach wissenschaftlicher Methode verfahrend] ...) argumentation

s/he	hypothesizes ([haɪ'pɒθɪsaɪzɪz], annehmen [als Hypothese]) that…
	works on the premise (mit der Annahme, Voraussetzung) that…

s/he presents	the thesis that…
	an antithesis [–'–––] to the view that…

The beginning of a piece of formal argumentation

The	common belief	is that…
	popular conception (Vorstellung)	

The usual assumption (Annahme)	is that…
One hypothesis	

With regard to *X*, one	problem is what to…
	problematic area is how to…

In a recent (kürzlich [erschienen])	paper	on *X*, *A*	has argued that…
	book		tried to demonstrate how…
			hypothesized that…

However, it can (may / might / …) (also) be argued that…
But it can be claimed (demonstrated / …) that…

The middle of a piece of formal argumentation

It is	admissible (zulässig)	to doubt (zweifeln) whether…
	permissible (statthaft)	

It is possible	to ask how…
	to dispute (in Frage stellen) the hypothesis that…
	to refute (widerlegen) the thesis that…

It is	appropriate (angemessen)	to suppose (vermuten) that…
	reasonable (vernünftig)	to claim (behaupten) that…
		to assert (behaupten) that…

The	point	can be illustrated from *B*'s discussion of…
	idea	

In his paper on *X*, *B* says, "..." [quotation] (cf. [title, place, year of publication, page])
In a chapter of *B*'s book on *X*, the point (question /...) is raised (aufwerfen) whether...
It says (Es heißt) in the text, [quote] "..." [unquote] (cf. pp ... ff.)

Another way of looking at the problem is to...
It is reasonable to assume that...
A convincing case can be made for *X*, if we examine the following data...

– use of causal clauses

Since (Da) we know from *C* that *X* is..., we can work with the hypothesis that...

(CF. "TEXT FORM DICTIONARY", 10, III.)

– use of conditional clauses

Even if we **limit** our investigation (Untersuchung) to..., there **will come** to light numerous instances (Fälle, Beispiele) of...

If we also **considered** the way *D* expresses himself in the play (novel /...), we **would be justified** in claiming that...

If *A* **had approached** (angehen) the passage (text / question / ...) from this angle (Blickwinkel), he **would have (might have / could have) found** that...

(CF. "TEXT FORM DICTIONARY", 10, IV.)

– use of concessive clauses

Although (Obwohl) a number of critics have disputed the possibility that *X* could mean... (cf., for instance, *C* and *D*), I would here like to suggest that...

(CF. "TEXT FORM DICTIONARY", 10, IV.)

– the -ing form with a subject of its own

A, for instance, strongly disagrees | **with us saying** that...
| **with *B* claiming** that...

For similar reasons, I am opposed **to *A* accepting** as evidence what can clearly be dismissed (abweisen) as...

– use of viewpoint (Blickwinkel) adverbs

Strictly (Genau [gesagt]), Lexically (Den Wortschatz betreffend), Stylistically (Stilistisch [gesehen]), Linguistically (Sprachlich [betrachtet]),	the text poses (aufwerfen) the problem whether...

Scientifically (Wissenschaftlich [methodisch]), Technically (Fachlich [gesehen]),	it can be	argued demonstrated	that...

Ideologically (Ideologisch [gesehen]), *A* does not explain why...

The end of a piece of formal argumentation

To conclude, In conclusion,	it seems probable (wahrscheinlich) that...

So, we still lack (haben keine) conclusive (schlüssig) evidence concerning the question whether...

In conclusion, it might be said that *X* is the key	to the explanation of... to our understanding of... to our interpretation of...

Having considered (Nachdem wir betrachtet haben) the major objections (Haupteinwände) to the assumption that...,	we may say... it seems safe to postulate (behaupten, postulieren) that...

As a result, *X* is...

It is clear, then, that	basically in its basic nature	our interpretation of *X*	is appropriate... is suited... (to describing /...)

Evidently (Offensichtlich), such a conception is in agreement with...

It	agrees with... corresponds to... (steht in Übereinstimmung mit) does not conflict with... (steht nicht in Widerspruch zu)

12. Personal instructions and practical or statutory instruction

Talking about instructive texts

Someone has his instructions (Anweisungen) to do *X*
These are his / her instructions concerning *X*
s/he follows the instructions for use (Gebrauchsanweisungen)

s/he	reads	the instruction book (Bedienungsanleitung)
	studies	the recipe (['resɪpɪ], Rezept) for...

s/he is / has been instructed to do *X*

s/he	follows	his / her	orders
	obeys		instructions
			directions (Anweisungen)

I. Personal instructions

The beginning of personal instructions

– addressing myself/ourselves

I	would like (möchte gern)	to do *X*
	want	
	mean (vorhaben)	
	intend (beabsichtigen)	
	plan	

I wish (wünschte) I	had...
	were in...
	could do *X*

I	have to	do *X*
	must	
	must not (darf nicht)	

I have been	asked	to do *X*
	told	
	instructed (anweisen)	
	urged (bedrängen)	
	exhorted ([ɪg'zɔ:tɪd], ermahnen)	

I am	expected to (man erwartet, daß ich)	do *X*
	meant to (ich soll)	
	intended to (soll)	

I have been	requested (höflich bitten)	to do *X*
	begged (immer wieder dringend bitten)	
	implored (anflehen)	

It is my	duty (Pflicht)	to do sth.
	obligation (Verpflichtung)	

I	am under an obligation to do *X*
	have the right to sth.
	am entitled (berechtigt) to do sth.

– *use of the auxiliary "be to"*

I	am to do *X* (soll, auf Anordnung oder nach Vereinbarung)
	am not to do *Y*

– *use of the auxiliaries "should" and "ought to"*

I	should	do *X* (sollte eigentlich)
	should not	

I should begin by doing *X*

I	ought	to do	*X*
	ought not		*Y*
	oughtn't		

– *use of the auxiliaries "had better/best" and "had/would rather"*

I	had better (würde besser)	do *X*
	had best (würde am besten)	not do *Y*

I	had rather (möchte lieber, eher) do *X* first
	would rather not do *Y* now

I	promise (versprechen)	to do *X*
	pledge (feierlich versprechen)	not to do *Y*
	swear (schwören)	

– *use of the future tense with "will", "shall", "'ll"*

I	will	try to do *X*
	shall [ʃəl]	

I'll	do *X*
I won't (will not)	do *Y*

– use of the future with "going to"

I am going to (vorhaben) do *X* now

– addressing others

Please,	do *X*
	don't do *Y*

Could	you do *X* (for me / us)?
Would	

Could you be	so nice and do *X*?
	so kind and do *Y*?
	so kind as to do *X* again?

I'd be much obliged (to you) (wäre [Ihnen] sehr zu Dank verpflichtet) if you could do *X*

– use of "you" plus "to"-infinitive

Can	I ask you to do *X* (for me / us)?
May (Darf)	
Might (Dürfte)	

I	would like	you to do *X*
	beg	

I	request (höflich bitten)	you to do *X*
	urge (drängen)	
	implore (anflehen)	

I	desire (sehr wünschen)	you to do *X*
	want	
	expect	
	intend	

I	tell ask (auffordern) order (befehlen) instruct (anweisen) command (befehlen)	you to do *X*

– use of auxiliaries

You	should ought to (solltest [auf Grund moralischer Verpflichtung]) are to (sollst [auf Grund einer bestehenden Anordnung])	do *X*

You	will want are well advised (gut beraten sein)	to do *X*

I would	advise (raten) counsel (raten)	you to do *X*

I	suggest (vorschlagen) propose (vorschlagen) recommend (empfehlen)	that you do *X*

You	can could may might	do *X* before you.../when you...

You are	asked (aufgefordert werden) told instructed directed (angewiesen werden) exhorted (ermahnt werden)	to do *X*

You are	expected (man erwartet, daß) meant intended	to do *X*

It is your duty to do *X*
You are under a (n) (moral) obligation not to do *Y*

The middle of personal instructions

– addressed to myself/ourselves

First	I	would like	to do *X*
Then		mean (beabsichtigen)	to do *Y/Z/...*
Next		intend	
Last (ly)		plan	

First, I shall do *X*
Second, I will (werde) do *Y*
Third, I am going to (vorhaben) do *Z*

– addressed to others

First (Then/Next/Last), I	would like	you to do *X*
	intend	

First, (Second,/...) you	should	do *X*
	ought to	

– use of imperative sentences

Do *X*
Don't do *Y*

You do *X*, and you (over there) do *Y*

Be careful	to	do *X* (Achtet darauf, daß)
	not to	

Be	prepared (vorbereitet)	to do *Y*
	ready (bereit)	

Have	*X*	ready
Keep		on hand (zur Hand)

The end of personal instructions

Last	I want you to do *X*
Lastly	you are expected to do *Y*
Finally	you should do *Z*

And fifth	you are intended (sollst) to do *X* and *Y*
Fifth and lastly,	

II. Practical instruction

The beginning of practical instruction

You should begin by (doing *X* / not doing *Y*)
First do *X*
First, don't do *Y*

Take Run through (Durchlaufe)	the following (four/five/...) steps: ...

Be ready to	observe (beachten) the following obey (befolgen) these	conventions rules maxims (Grundregeln) principles (Grundsätze)

You want to follow these	precepts (Leitlinien) guidelines (Richtlinien)

The middle of practical instruction

First, ... (1. .../...)
Second, ... (2. .../...)

It may be	useful necessary (notwendig) advisable (ratsam) wise (klug)	to do *X*

It is	inadvisable (nicht ratsam) unwise	to do *Y*

It is a good idea to do *Z* (first)

The next	step (Schritt) stage (Stufe)	could be to do *X*

In another (einem weiteren) step, In your next step,	you	should do have to must do	*Y*

– use of clauses with "where" (local clauses)

Where the *X* is,	you should do *Y*
Where you see *X*,	

You should not do *X* **where (***A* and *B* meet [sich treffen] /…)

– use of clauses with "when", etc. (time clauses)

When you do *X*,	watch out for (gib Acht auf)
	be careful not to …
	have *B* ready for …

Before you	add *X*,	you should do *Y*
	take the next step,	

As soon as (Sobald) you have finished doing *X*, you can go on to do *Y*

After doing *X*, take the next step

– use of clauses with "if", etc. (conditional clauses)

If you	want to	do *X*, do *Y* first (next/…)
	have to	

Unless (Wenn nicht) you can be sure that *X* has been	done,	you should not do …
	fixed,	
	written,	
	read,	

As long as (Solange, Sofern) *X* is clear (safe /…), you can do *Y*

– use of clauses with "so that" (purposive clauses)

Remember	to do *X*, **so that** *Y* can be done
Do not forget	

To do *X*,	consult (zu Rate ziehen) a	dictionary
To write a clear paragraph,		guide to writing
To divide a word,		special handbook

To ensure (sicherstellen)	*X*,	you should (always) do *Y*
	clarity (Klarheit),	
	accuracy (Richtigkeit),	

If you use	*X*,	do *Y*	**so as to** (um zu) show what (the original words are)
	quotations,	put square brackets (eckige Klammern) around words you yourself add to the quotation,	**in order to** avoid (confusion [Verwirrung] /...)

For doing	*X*,	do not use (your pen /...)
	correcting misspelt words,	

– use of clauses with "by doing" (manner clauses)

By	**doing** *X*,	you can show	where (a new paragraph begins /...)
	indenting lines (Zeilen einrücken),		

You can help your reader **by**	doing *X*
	adding headings (Überschriften) to your paper

The end of practical instruction

Last,	you should do *X*
Lastly,	
Finally,	

And fifth,	do *Y*
Fifth and lastly,	

III. Statutory instruction

The beginning of reported (berichtete) statutory instruction

In the (Education/...) Act of 19..,	it says that (heißt es, daß) *X* is to be done
	the following provisions (Vorkehrungen, Bestimmungen) are made ...

The	rules	say that ...
	regulations (Regelungen)	demand that ...
		require all *X*s to do *Y*

The treaty (Vertrag) of 18..	laid down (legte fest)	that no *X*	should be (used)
	guaranteed		were to be sold

The statutes (Gesetze) on *X* lay down that …

A (nineteenth /…) century	law ruling ordinance (Verordnung)	stipulated (verlangte) that no *X* should … / was to …

According to (Nach) article *X*, section *Y* of the constitution, no *Z* is to be (sold / elected /…) without …

The middle of reported statutory instruction

The act of 19.. That measure (Maßnahme) The provisions (Vorkehrungen) of this act	authorized (ermächtigen) empowered	the president (prime minister / king / …) to do *X*

That measure made it	legal legally binding mandatory (zwingend verordnet)	that … (had to /…)

It is	legitimate [lɪˈdʒɪtɪmɪt], lawful (rechtmäßig) legal (gesetzlich zulässig)	for *A* to do *X*

People are not	allowed permitted (erlauben)	to do *X*

They	must must not (dürfen nicht)	do *X*

All groups mentioned in this measure (regulation /…) are to be (sollen)	given (erhalten) granted (bewilligen) guaranteed	the right to …

It	was became	unlawful illegal	to do *X*

Parliament Congress	enacted (per Gesetz anordnen) passed (verabschieden)	a law to … a law that …

Congress legislated	for (the rights of ...) against (the practices of /...)

The legislative body of (the state of ...) The legislature (gesetzgebende Körperschaft) The legislator (Gesetzgeber)	repealed (aufheben) the	controversial (umstritten) / unpopular /... (Rent Act)

The legislator has	maintained upheld enforced (Geltung verschaffen)	the law that ...

The	treaty ([öffentlicher] Vertrag) contract ([privater] Vertrag)	was annulled (aufheben) by a court ruling (Gerichtsentscheid) saying that ...

The	law statute	forbids sb. (him / her) to do *X*

The government has	banned (untersagen) outlawed (für ungesetzlich erklären)	all *X*s

Doing *X* is prohibited (verboten) (by law)

Books Films Newspapers	have been censored (['sensəd], zensieren) are under censorship (unterliegen der Zensur)

The end of reported statutory instruction

The Act was	passed signed	by ...

The Treaty	bears has	the signatures (Unterschriften) of ...

The signatory powers (Unterzeichnermächte) to the	agreement treaty	of *X* were ...